BULLY & THE BADGER

WICKHAM MALINS

BULLY & THE BADGER

with drawings by
Eileen A. Soper

foreword by Ernest G. Neal

Robert Yeatman Ltd 1974

For my wife and family
with love from their
old badger bore

First published 1974 by Robert Yeatman Ltd
401 Grand Buildings, Trafalgar Square
London WC2N 5HD

Designed by Melvyn Gill Design Associates
Photoset by Amos Typesetters Ltd
Printed in Great Britain by New Avenue Press Ltd

ISBN 0 903590 05 0

ACKNOWLEDGEMENTS

I should like to express my thanks to the many people who have, in one way or another, been involved in the production of this book and without whose help it would never have seen the light of day. I am particularly grateful to Mrs E. Jane Ratcliffe for the invaluable advice she gave when by chance it fell to me to bring up Jess, to Jeremy Stockley and Peter Ford for their help in putting the story together and to Joyce Way for her patient typing of my innumerable manuscripts. My gratitude also extends to Arthur Talbot and Peter Hogg for the many photographs they took, only some of which have been reproduced, and to Miss Eileen Soper for her delightful drawings.

Apart from those who are mentioned in the story, I feel the Bully and I should also record our appreciation to all our kindly neighbours, especially those over whose land we may have at some time trespassed.

Lastly, and by no means least, I must acknowledge my indebtedness to Dr Ernest Neal. He has not only written a Foreword to the book and offered his advice and kindly criticism, but, unknowingly, first aroused my interest in badgers and taught me all that I knew about these delightful animals before I became involved in rearing one.

Old Farm Place
Battle
Sussex

C.W.M.

CONTENTS

FOREWORD

Badgers are no longer the mysterious animals they once were. Ignorance and prejudice about them still lingers, but with most people today the badger is looked upon with interest and affection as the ancient Briton he undoubtedly is. A landowner in his own right for more than a quarter of a million years in this country, the badger excites our admiration for the way he is coping with life in the twentieth century.

It is not always an easy life for badgers today. Many are killed on the roads or electrocuted on the railways, others are snared in case they should do damage to man's interests. But badgers are adaptable creatures and they are learning to co-exist with a greatly expanding human population.

Badger cubs have been reared as pets by many people—a few people have even written stories about their experiences. Fortunately, it is now illegal to bring them up as pets, for the charming cuddly cub soon grows into a strong and often destructive adult and the disillusioned foster parent is soon wondering what can be done to restore peace in the home. Zoos usually have plenty of badgers already, and to turn a tame one loose in the country, even if it has learned to fend for itself, can be disastrous, as the wild badgers on whose territory it is released may maul or even kill it.

This charming story of Jess, a rescued badger cub, has a very different ending–different because she was respected from the start as a wild animal, but one which needed human understanding and help before returning to her own wild heritage.

It is no easy matter bringing up a wild animal in this way: you are apt to become too fond of it–to treat it as something to be enjoyed and humanized. But if this temptation can be resisted, the reward is far more satisfying.

The story is a true one and is told with humour and understanding. The reader quickly feels involved, as if he were one of the family, and in the process learns much about badgers. It is a pleasure to commend this book to all who have regard for the wildlife of this country.

Ernest Neal
September 1974

1
A WEEKEND WALK

But any man that walks the mead
In bud or blade or bloom, may find,
According to his humour's lead
A meaning suited to his mind.
Alfred Lord Tennyson

My family were thoroughly bored with badgers because–to use the idiom of the day–they had me 'hooked'. I cannot really blame them, for most of my walks in winter were invariably related to a visit to a badger sett and in summer I often used to go out by myself to watch them in the evenings.

Although I had always been interested in wild animals and had, with my wife Gill, one sunny evening in Hereford, seen badger cubs at play, my knowledge of these intriguing creatures was very limited until we moved our home to Sussex. I had by then more or less retired from the sea, and it came as something of a surprise to find that we were living in an area that was comparatively thickly populated with them. I soon learnt where to find their setts and was gradually able to recognize the evidence which they leave of their various activities at night, when they come out in search of food. Our weekend walks would be interrupted while, to my family's exasperation, I used to investigate a badger latrine. This is an essential occupation to the serious badger student, since the shallow little dung-pits, which they usually dig within a stone's throw of their sett, contain many useful clues to their secret and little-known life.

Before long, I knew the location of some thirty setts in the immediate neighbourhood, and had a fair idea of whether or not they were being occupied at any particular time. Visitors to Old Farm Place would frequently be cajoled or persuaded into climbing up a tree, in which they would be expected to sit without sound or movement for long stretches of time, enduring the bites of midges.

All in all, however, my hobby had never really won much appreciation from Gill and our large and outspoken family until the year when Jess entered all our lives.

It all began with a casual remark by one of my oldest friends, who was spending a long weekend with us in the middle of April, when we were chatting about the Isle of Man, where he recently had retired. 'We have no foxes or badgers on the island,' he said that Saturday. 'In fact, I've never seen a badger in my life.'

There was a shocked and unbelieving silence in the room where we were sitting with Gill and our two younger daughters, Priscilla and Joanna.

'Never seen a badger?' said Gill, a tone of pity in her voice which might well have been interpreted as a warning.

'Have I said something terrible?' he asked.

'Yes, though it all depends what you mean by terrible,' came the unanimous reaction from my family as they saw what he was letting himself in for.

'Well, before you leave us, you shall see one,' I promised him, 'and we'll improve your education.'

There were immediate expressions of sympathy from Gill and the two girls, all of whom had witnessed the further education of many guests in the past. For some while I had felt that our younger daughters, who were still resident in the family, had not been paying the full respect due to me as head of the household. With their eldest sister married and their three brothers earning their livings away from home and no longer able to back me up, they were having things altogether too much their own way. I had begun to suspect some sort of conspiracy between them and their mother to cure me somehow of my addiction, in the mistaken belief that badgers had become a threat to my mental equilibrium. So it was something of a relief to have my old friend Roland Watkin staying with us, who, for as long as I could remember, had been affectionately known to all his friends as Basher, on account of his pugilistic appearance. His presence was doing much to reinforce my position as the only male in the family.

Basher and I had many interests in common apart from our earlier careers at sea. He also enjoyed long country walks and shared my fascination in wild animals, of which we had seen many different species on our visits to distant parts of the world. About badgers, on the other hand, he clearly knew very little. I felt certain that the prospect of some outdoor activity would have his support and that he would welcome the chance of seeing something new, even if it only turned out to be a few holes in the ground.

As the girls began to decry my eccentricities and to warn him of the discomforts that lay ahead, I knew that they were only making it the more likely that Basher would accept the challenge. As the pattern of conversation unfolded that morning, I therefore took no further part and held my peace. Nothing had ever daunted Basher in the past and no greater champion of a good cause could be found. I was also confident that he would see through the wiles of my daughters since he had two of his own and had, for many years, successfully assumed the role of consort to the headmistress of a well-known boarding school for girls.

Basher had lost none of his former spirit and told the girls not to underestimate their father and himself, simply because we were no longer dressed in bell-bottoms. Then, wiping his copious brow, he stalked out of the room to tap the cider barrel for the third time in twenty minutes. Was it thirst, I wondered, or nerves?

When he came back, however, I thought there was just the hint of a retreat in his suggestion that perhaps we might make it an afternoon walk instead. After all, it was abnormally warm for the time of the year, and was there not a good chance that a badger might be found sunning itself outside its sett? As if to add weight to his argument, he took another quick, if superfluous, mop of his brow and shot an astute glance in my direction to see if I was reading his thoughts aright.

'You see,' said Basher, 'with luck it might possibly save two old sailors like us from some unnecessary gymnastics and an evening pantomime in the boughs of a tree.'

As he said this I had visions of having to hoist his not inconsiderable weight high into the tree, and hopefully in silence. The rule of no talking, however cold or however cramped we might become, would undoubtedly tax his loquacious and irrepressible spirit beyond its natural limits, for he would have to wait quietly for at least an hour if he wanted to see any badgers.

People who have never watched badgers must wonder what prompts the enthusiasm of badger watchers to suffer these discomforts at any time of the year when trying to see the almost invisible in the dark. It's not an easy question to answer: like other country pastimes which require a certain amount of endurance, you simply have to get the urge. Much patience must be evoked and disappointment endured to gain even a brief glimpse of these shy nocturnal animals. Once the glimpse is achieved, however, the excitement takes over, crowding out all other thoughts as you cease to notice the cold, cramp or tormenting insects. There is a challenge also in trying to overcome the badger's wary instincts and well-developed fear of human beings. This fear is not surprising when you consider how, for centuries, humans have persecuted badgers, and how their only natural predator has been man, and perhaps his dog.

My one preoccupation at that particular moment, however, was wondering whether Basher would get the necessary urge, and if he did, what the chances might be of his sustaining it throughout a lengthy vigil? He no longer had quite the agile figure he had had when I first knew him in his youth. The spirit was still there, certainly, but we would need to become tree-borne for the evening to be rewarding and I began to suspect that his usual clear thinking was already foreseeing all the problems.

The hope of actually stumbling on a badger basking in the sun at that time of the year, however warm the day, seemed to me extremely remote. Badgers only rarely make appearances in daytime, though sometimes during the summer months they may be seen sunning themselves outside their setts around midday. Evening or early before sunrise are undoubtedly the best times for watching badgers, particularly during May or June. Then, if there are any young ones about and the sett is in a remote area, they may often be seen playing for quite long periods before they go off to forage for food with their parents.

Badger cubs often seem to have no natural fear of humans, and sometimes, in the absence of their parents, will fearlessly approach and sniff a watcher's shoes. Fear of man is something that young badgers must subsequently be taught by their parents or learn for themselves by experience. If they do come close, and are not frightened by any sudden movement, it can be quite easy to feed them with such delicacies as honey and raisins, to which they are very partial. But it was still only April and very unlikely that the year's cubs would yet be old enough to venture above ground during daylight.

'Very well, Basher,' I said at last. 'We'll take a badger walk this afternoon, and we can rehearse for a stretch of "watching" this evening, to see how you feel about it.'

There was an expectant pause in the conversation, but no other volunteers came forward. Basher, obviously hoping he might have had the company of Priscilla and Joanna, looked at me with some misgivings. Suddenly he thumped the table with his now empty tankard, signifying a mind decisively made up. 'We'll go this minute,' he said with enthusiasm, 'while the sun is not yet over the yardarm, and you will show me a badger that can't resist its warmth.'

I imagined at the time that his main objective was to get the matter over and so spend the evening comfortably at home by the fire. In view of what happened, however, I wondered afterwards whether he was not displaying a gift for clairvoyance that he had until then been too modest to disclose. So it was that we set out, if not at that very moment, immediately after lunch.

On my walks I was invariably accompanied by my bull-terrier, Dinah, who despite an impressive name registered with the Kennel Club, was more commonly known to my family as 'the Bully' because of her long-standing aversion to grey squirrels. She rarely strayed far away, and was not in the least interested in pheasants or other birds, but she had a very sharp eye for squirrels, which she would harry unmercifully whenever they were seen or scented and which she had, on many occasions, managed to catch and kill. All bull-terriers tend to have their obsessions, but apart from a hatred for all squirrels Dinah had a very equable temperament and should never really have been called a bully. It was a complete misnomer. She would answer to either name, however, provided it suited her pleasure, and was always amusing company.

After years of walks with me, Dinah soon learnt to devote at least some of her attention to the badger setts we visited. She would naturally follow up any part of their extensive system of paths which we came across, and had often led me to setts that I might not otherwise have found. Once in a sett, it was her custom to stick just her nose down the various entrances–fortunately she could go no further–and either wag her tail or give a little snort if she thought the occupants were at home. Thus the Bully had obviously come to know something about badgers, though as far as I was aware she had never met one face to face and I had often wondered what would happen if she did. One day we had met another bull-terrier in Friston Forest who had had a fight with a badger the previous evening and seemed to have come off second best. There were ugly bites about his throat and jaw which had had to be stitched.

Our only other companion on the walk that afternoon was Gill's Jack Russell (another female in the family), who like all members of her breed could boast no pedigree and was simply known as Trottie Wagtail; so named because her behaviour resembled so clearly that of the bird in John Clare's poem. Although she too was good fun to have on a walk, Trottie was frequently an embarrassment owing to a regrettable tendency to complete deafness whenever her nose detected something interesting. So she had to be kept strictly on a lead, on which she pulled like mad whenever there was the slightest opportunity of slipping off among the brambles or of going to ground.

Feeling for all the world as if summer had arrived that sunny April afternoon, we had started off at a brisk pace towards an area, some two and a half miles away, which I knew was particularly thickly populated with badgers. The farm I intended visiting had several large setts, one of which I had watched regularly throughout the previous year from a near-by oak tree, in which I had fitted a suitable seat. After we had gone a short distance, however, I noticed Basher was not particularly well shod. We therefore agreed to return discreetly and cover some of the distance by car, since it would give us more time to look at all the other setts in the area.

Once we had exchanged greetings with the farmer, who had often laughed uproariously at my interest in his badgers, but had kindly stored my ladder in his barn during winter, we set out towards the woods, with Trottie firmly on the lead. The Bully, of course, knew the area extremely well and rushed eagerly ahead, her eyes, as always, on the trees. As we still had some way to go, I thought it would be wise to prime Basher on the true facts of the badger-watching life and what he might expect when and if we returned later that evening.

Badgers can easily detect the approach or presence of human beings through their acute sense of smell and hearing. This means that the would-be watcher must silently take up his position well before the inmates of a sett have woken and are ready to emerge. In a wood, where the wind is often fitful, you must if possible get at least six feet above the ground; this will give a far better view over a much wider area, if not of the whole sett, and your scent will probably drift clear. No camouflage or special hide is then necessary, since badgers have very little interest in birds and naturally neither suspect nor anticipate danger from above.

When he first emerges from his day-long sleep, shortly before or after sunset, a badger will usually just poke his nose out to test the wind, and will in all likelihood do this several times before feeling satisfied that the coast is clear. Thus assured, he will probably relax his guard a little and venture further out to be followed by others. Some families of badgers may become accustomed to the scent of a particular person around their sett when they find they are in no way molested, but they will never really be at ease unless completely unaware of the presence of intruders.

Once they are sure that all is well, badgers often spend a long time grooming themselves and particularly their cubs, with whom the parents often play, though they will not usually emerge until well after dusk when the cubs are still young. If the sett is in a quiet area and they are not disturbed, badgers may often be observed in daylight in the summer months, gathering bedding and generally attending to their domestic chores before going off in search of food. However, they instinctively dislike strong daylight and will rarely leave the cover of woods or hedgerows until it is quite dark.

On account of this, I explained to Basher, we might have to use a torch later, and I would bring one with a red filter, because, for some reason, badgers do not seem to mind red light. From up a tree it is sometimes possible to use a torch that throws a diffused white light, which they presumably mistake for the moon, but a strong beam directed straight at a badger from ground level will immediately send it bolting down the sett.

To the point as always, Basher now suggested it was I who was talking too much, for we were nearing the sett and he could see my rustic ladder leaning against the tree. 'As they say in Australia,' he remarked, as we carefully anchored Trottie some way off, 'you've got a dinkum piece of bush carpentry here.' We quietly approached the tree. After he had inspected the scantlings of the ladder with his seaman's eye, I proposed that we climb up and carry out a 'dummy run'. Basher hesitated; I assured him that my family had often been up the ladder with me; a statement Gill and Priscilla later diluted by saying that they had only ever done so because of a sense of loyalty and under protest. So, to give him a lead, I climbed up quickly and settled myself on a second seat for visitors that I had previously fitted on one of the branches. It soon became obvious that, although he was still hoping that we might see a badger in the middle of the afternoon, it was not so much the strength of the ladder which was worrying Basher as the prospect of having to hoist himself, even with the aid of a rope, into the seat at the top.

'It's like going over the futtock shrouds of a square-rigged ship,' he grumbled as he clambered laboriously up the ladder, with much puffing and blowing. 'All very well for chaps shaped like a marlin spike,' he muttered as we finally settled ourselves in like a couple of old sailors in the crow's nest of an old-fashioned ship.

Apart from the sound of Basher recovering his breath, the noise of the Bully crashing around further up the wood in a search for squirrels and some cows lowing in the distance, all was silent. It was, as Basher described it later, 'One of those rare peaceful moments that has indelibly imprinted itself on my memory.' This was hardly fair since I was sitting precariously on a branch and he had by far the most comfortable seat; it even had arm-rests. For a while I thought he was settling down for the short siesta he had already foregone and seemed prepared for a lengthy vigil; but I was wrong and eventually realized that he was simply waiting for me to make the next move, being determined not to have to lead the descent himself.

We had, of course, made much too much noise for there to be any hope of seeing any badgers, even supposing one had had the intention of sun-bathing that afternoon. So I proposed we might clamber down, retrieve the waiting Trottie and continue the walk. Basher was, however, anxious to see all he could and suggested we might just carry out an inspection of the sett. This was against all my rules, for a badger will scent a human footstep many hours after the imprint has been made and I didn't want to spoil our chances of seeing some that evening. However, I eventually agreed, and we were cautiously approaching one of the entrances on the perimeter of the sett when, to my absolute amazement, we saw a baby badger slowly emerging out of a hole, only a few feet in front of us.

We froze. So, fortunately, did Trottie, who could not see the cub. It was a most thrilling moment. It was most unusual to see such a small cub out in daylight. We stood motionless and watched for some minutes as it staggered unsteadily out into the sunlight, sniffing and peering around.

The cub was completely unaware of our presence; it sat down and made half-hearted attempts at grooming itself, as grown-up badgers will. When suddenly, to my consternation, the Bully appeared as if from nowhere with her squirrel-hunting look. She was bounding through the trees as only a bull-terrier can; it was, of course, a squirrel hunter's paradise, and the fact that the leaves were only in bud had clearly raised her hopes of an engagement with the enemy. I hoped that one might miraculously appear from somewhere–but no such luck. She caught sight

of us instead and bounced cheerfully in our direction.

There seemed nothing that I could do to avert disaster. My commanding shout of 'Sit!' broke the fragile silence, but didn't disturb the cub. The Bully would never sit willingly when it didn't please her, especially when on a walk. Spotting the defenceless little cub below her inviting slaughter, and doubtless thinking it was her hated foe, for it was about the same size, she pounced with a yelp that made my heart stop beating. Encouraged by a now frantic Trottie, still on her lead at my heel, the Bully grabbed the unfortunate little cub firmly in her jaw right across the spine. It gave the most appalling scream of pain, which I knew meant death in seconds.

Quick decisions of one sort or another had all been part of our early naval training, and, right or wrong, we had been taught to see them through. Basher's and my memories of playing rugby football were pretty dim. In any case, being the wrong shape, I had never been much good at low flying tackles. Besides, I was wearing a kilt at the time, and kilts have never been recommended wear for rugby players or even for watching badgers. Yet I managed to gather up the yelping Trottie and fling her at the open-mouthed Basher as though she were the ball (he neatly accepting the pass) before diving through the air to tackle an angry Bully. I grabbed her tail with one hand and forced her mouth open with the other, and there, before me, cackling and shivering with fright, lay the smallest badger I had ever seen, which I swiftly gathered up to prevent further damage.

Basher meanwhile was managing to preserve an admirable sang-froid, despite a struggling Trottie. He later confessed that he had been much too absorbed in the whole hectic scene to have been of any use, and was anyway having visions of being nipped by a bull-terrier, a Jack Russell and a badger at one and the same time. It was, in fact, surprising that neither of us did get bitten in that brief mad scramble. But my mind had already moved on to the next part of the problem: what on earth should we do now?

As I saw the situation, there were two over-excited dogs at our feet and a badger cub, perhaps seven or eight weeks old, in my hands. Cubs of that age are, as a rule, entirely dependent on their mothers, so ought I to put it back down the hole, or first try and find out what damage the Bully had inflicted? A quick examination showed no obvious wound. There was evidently no blood, but the Bully's bite, of course, could have caused internal haemorrhage. To put the cub back could, I thought, be very risky; it would obviously now reek of both me and bull-terrier, which would almost certainly make it unacceptable to its mother and to other badgers. There was, I reasoned, nothing to do except take it home. In any case, it appeared to be extremely weak and we were both agreed that its chances of survival seemed slim whatever we did.

At this point I decided that the most sensible thing to do was to get rid of the dogs and put Basher in charge of the cub.

'Don't let it re-enter the sett, and mind it doesn't nip you,' I shouted over my shoulder as I made off towards the road; leaving Basher, who clearly was not relishing the prospect of being bitten by a badger, however weak and infantile, carefully guarding the cub between his feet.

When I returned, bringing an old blanket, he was in perfect control of the situation, with the little badger seemingly asleep and snuggled close against his shoes. It whimpered and cackled slightly as we gently placed it in the blanket; and, with the dogs safely secured on the back seat and the precious bundle on Basher's lap, reached home without further incident.

Gill was out when we got back.

'You've only seen half this drama,' I said to Basher, 'and will have to wait till she returns to see the rest.'

2
THE DILEMMA

'Twas the women, not the warriers, turned those
stark enthusiasts pale,
For the female of the species is more deadly
than the male.

Rudyard Kipling

Before anyone takes on the rearing of any wild creature, they should stop and remember that their responsibilities will not necessarily cease when the animal reaches adolescence. These are, in fact, very likely to extend into maturity, so it is not a task to be lightly undertaken.

Many wild animals are naturally attractive, and it is tempting to think that they can be brought up to become more or less fully domesticated members of a household. This is to forget, however, that the true domestic animals, including cats and dogs, have been bred by man over many thousands of years into what they are today. Wild young badger, fox or otter cubs can and have been successfully reared by hand, but the real problems start when their instincts, all of which relate to their natural habitat, begin to assert themselves. Then some people may feel that, once they have reached maturity, they can easily be put back in the wild; but unless the animal has been given some sort of training, it may well be at a severe disadvantage. Although instinct plays an important part, many vital lessons must be learned from their parents by most wild animals, who, among other things, have to be taught how to cope with the hostilities of their natural predators, which may often include members of their own species. It may sometimes be kinder and less selfish to let nature take its natural course in the first place.

It is certainly true that badger cubs reared by hand do make amusing and delightful pets. They can even be trained like a puppy, and I had read several accounts of cubs brought up by hand which made it all sound a reasonably easy task. In sentimental moments I had even hoped that such an opportunity might one day come my way, but, now that it had done so, I began to feel serious misgivings.

Most young mammals grow up very quickly and badgers are no exception. They are more or less full grown when nine months old, and their nocturnal and other habits do moreover present peculiar problems. If their well-developed clannish and territorial instinct is interfered with too drastically it can have disastrous consequences. A captive badger is said to be capable of displaying voracious energy and persistence in escaping from surroundings which it finds uncongenial. Then, despite the fact that badgers are generally inoffensive creatures who mind their own business and seek no quarrel with any other animal (unless it is another badger) their bite is notoriously vicious. Although their mouths are comparatively small, they are well equipped with teeth and have exceedingly strong muscles that exert considerable leverage on the jawbone, which is articulated in the skull so that it cannot dislocate. It has been said that a badger's teeth can even mark a spade.

I knew that Gill had heard grim tales of this, and that they can have unpredictable tempers when fully grown and mature. She had never concealed her total opposition whenever I had musingly said it might perhaps be interesting one day to add a badger to our family menagerie. Since I have to be away at work on weekdays, there would have been no hope of my doing so without her full co-operation.

All these thoughts, and many more, raced through my mind as Basher and I locked up the still-excited dogs and gently carried the little cub up to the barn. The girls were out riding at the time, so we carefully laid it in some straw in an empty stable before retiring to assess the situation more calmly over a cup of tea. As we sipped our tea, I wondered whether Basher would be any help as mediator in the storm that would inevitably shortly break about our heads when Gill came home.

'Many times she's told me I would have to choose between living with her or a badger,' I said.

'That will make an interesting choice,' was his only comment.

We thought it most likely that the cub was either ill or undernourished, and agreed that it did not seem to have suffered any serious harm from its unfortunate encounter with the Bully. So far as we could tell, no bones had been broken, and it seemed still able to stagger a little, as before. As we talked, I prepared some warm diluted milk and laced it generously with glucose. This we took to the cub, where it lay helpless and exhausted in the absent pony's bedding. It did not seem to be in the least afraid, and even licked a little liquid from my fingers. Thus reassured, we resumed our conference over the tea-pot.

By this time I had convinced myself that if the cub were to be taken straight back to the sett, it would, after all our handling, certainly be rejected by its family. Since it was obviously so weak we decided that the wisest thing would be to keep it and try feeding it for a day or so to help it regain strength.

This was the state of play when Gill returned home. We must have been on our third cup of tea at least, when she came into the kitchen and casually asked if we had had an interesting afternoon. To this we gave a rather non-commital answer, which was followed by an embarrassing silence. A gap in the conversation was rare indeed whenever Basher was in the house, so her suspicions were aroused at once.

'What have you two been up to?' she demanded.

'Well . . . nothing much,' we replied as one.

'Oh yes you have,' she said. 'I can tell by the looks on your faces.' So bit by bit we came out with the whole story.

'I knew this would happen one day. You will just have to go and put it back,' Gill said, looking straight and hard in my direction. 'At once.' Basher, ever a quick tactician, moved in to lay a smoke screen and draw the hostile fire in his direction.

'It was an absolute accident,' he said. 'You mustn't be too hard on him. He's only done a splendid one-man R.S.P.C.A. act.'

From that moment Basher was on his own and had to brace himself to meet the squall with only a teacup in his hand. Gill stood over him, gripping the back of his chair, and summoned all her latent histrionic powers to declare: 'It's all been your fault, Basher. This would never have happened if you hadn't suggested the walk, so you have got to persuade him to go and take it back.' To emphasize the finality of her judgement, she stamped so hard on the floor that Basher momentarily flinched. At that moment Priscilla and Joanna arrived home, and naturally joined in the argument; in loyal support of their mother, of course. It must be Basher's fault, they said, so it was up to him to do something about it.

Leaving Basher stoically and nobly weathering the mounting storm, I slipped quietly out of the room to prepare a little bowl of cornflakes with honey and warm milk. As I went off to the stables, I could hear him tactfully telling the girls that later in the evening would, he felt, be a better time for him to raise the subject with me again.

I knew I could rely on him to put up a heroic rearguard action, and, more than that, was sure he would eventually persuade them to come and see the poor helpless little creature for themselves. Once that happened, the day would be won. And so it came about: one look was enough.

'We must,' the girls all said, as if they had hit on an original idea, 'get it well before we return it to the sett.'

·ked a little liquid from my fingers'

'Allowed them both back into the house'

'The most devoted and possessive of foster mothers'

sting the wind

m the garden sett

With Lesley Judd *(By kind permission of the BBC)*

Later that evening, when we were offering the cub further diluted milk, which it then seemed able to lap with a little difficulty, the strangest thing happened. The Bully, knowing that I was inside the stable, came whining to the door asking me to let her in. I shall never know what flash of inspiration prompted me to do so, but I decided to introduce her to the new arrival on an altogether more civilized footing than their first encounter. The Bully had never had any pups of her own, though she was usually very amiable with other young animals. Having taken the precaution of putting her on a lead, I led her quietly into the stable. She was tensed with excitement, but slowly approached the frail little cub she had earlier tried to murder. She stood over it for a moment, giving it a preliminary but friendly sniff, and then, to everyone's amazement, lay down without further hesitation and offered it the use of her dairy, despite the fact that she had never had any milk. Obviously, she was sorry for her earlier misdeed. The cub responded with alacrity to the generous maternal gesture and set to with gusto and much noisy sucking, which not only showed that it lacked food, as we already suspected, but also that it was still entirely dependent on its mother.

That evening, gathered round the supper table, there was naturally only one topic of conversation. Everyone had a different theory. What was it that had brought such a young cub out of its sett alone in the middle of a sunny afternoon at a time when badgers normally sleep? Why was it so hungry and weak? Had it been rejected, or was it the runt pushed out by the stronger members of a litter? Could the family have moved for some reason, and left it behind, or had something happened to the mother? We would probably never know the answers, but were all agreed that the reason why the cub had at first seemed so ill was probably because it was starving.

The Bully was still a maiden, and only a few months before we had had to decide whether or not to go through with a plan to have her mated for the first time. However, the vet had advised that, in view of the fact she was five years old and that bull-terriers are a heavily boned breed, she might not experience an easy confinement. Mating might therefore have serious risks for her and could lead to the need for a caesarian birth. Since we knew very well that the Bully had a strong, ingrained dislike of all vets, that had clinched the matter. The decision to deny her the chance of rearing puppies was very much on our minds and we were all agreed that, if she seriously wanted to adopt the little cub, which in turn seemed so obviously glad of her company, we had no right to prevent or discourage her from doing so. At least the cub seemed able to lap a little liquid and we could always give it a bottle if necessary. It was therefore unanimously decided that we should let things take their natural course.

Our neighbours and visitors could seldom make head or tail of the animal goings-on at Old Farm Place. Basher was an honourable exception to this rule, since his family had a similar weakness. But, to others, we always seemed to be sheltering an astonishing range of animals stretching well beyond those generally accepted as normal domestic pets. It was quite likely that sick lambs disowned by their mothers, or fledgling Java doves, would greet anyone who arrived in the house or garden, so that those who knew us well became in time surprised at nothing.

By common consent, each animal had to be suitably named. So the cub must have a name as well. Our lambs were always called after biblical characters, and Gill's bantams after types of material. Our bull-terriers were, incidentally, all Romanies. The girls felt sure that 'Basher the Badger' would be just right, but the original owner of the name objected very strongly. Perhaps, he suggested, we ought to establish its sex before deciding on a name and, having satisfied himself that the cub had no sharp or vicious teeth, insisted that it was a matter on which he would need no advice and would like to carry out unaided. We all remained seated as he quietly rose from the table and went out to the stables.

He seemed to take an unconscionable time over such a simple little investigation. I pictured him stumbling about in the twilight, dropping or treading on the poor unfortunate cub, and began to wonder whether he should have been allowed to go alone. However, he returned eventually and sat down at the table, looking very glum. He did not say a word for a full minute and a sense of alarm was mounting. 'Well?' I asked, to break the tension.

'Bad news,' he grunted.

'How bad?' 'What's happened?' 'Is it dead?' Gill, Priscilla and Joanna all spoke together, while I, knowing Basher better, tried to appear unconcerned. Another dramatic pause; and he leaned forward across the table towards me, his hand up to his mouth as if to impart some specially confidential information.

'It's another girl,' he whispered.

So that was the end of Basher the Badger and the advent of Jess, for the cub was immediately named after Basher's devoted wife–a compliment and distinction we hoped she might in due course appreciate. When Basher wrote to confirm her consent a short while later, he hinted that his gifts in diplomacy had yet again been needed before 'she only reluctantly agreed to have the word badger associated with the name of a headmistress'.

Watered-down cow's milk is not highly suitable for most young animals, so we began feeding Jess on the same powdered milk we used for sock lambs, with a little sugar or glucose added. The Bully was allowed to suckle her whenever she felt inclined, with the result that she spent most of the next day with her strange foster-cub in the stable and, when they were separated fussed so much that, after a day or so, we allowed her to spend the nights there as well.

Although Jess was very lame for several days, and only able to hobble painfully about she quickly began to regain strength and was soon inseparable from the Bully, who she would follow faithfully anywhere in the garden or the

house. The two of them seemed so happy and contented together that Gill eventually relented and allowed them both back into the house with the use of the Bully's own bed in the kitchen. The Bully, in her turn, became the most devoted and possessive of foster mothers you could imagine.

All this, however, was not the end of our amazement. Within a week the most extraordinary thing of all occurred. The Bully gradually came into milk and was soon able to suckle Jess properly, having all the milk she required. What was even more surprising was that within ten days she was producing far more than one little badger could possibly consume. It seemed as though nature had stimulated the hormones which allowed the Bully to satisfy her maternal instincts to the full; something we gathered, that is very rare in maiden bitches, if not exactly unique.

It was some weeks before evidence came forward to show that Jess had most probably been an orphan and so was possibly the strongest and not the weakest of her litter. One evening, a friend of Pricilla's and Joanna's rode over to visit us, and seeing Jess lying in the basket with the Bully, casually asked where she had been found. On being told she said: 'Oh, that's funny; I saw a dead badger by the roadside near there some time ago when going to school.' She was, in fact, able to remember the exact date since it had been the last day of school before the Easter holidays had begun. This chance information set our minds at rest, for then we knew practically for certain that we *had* done the right thing after all. Later visits to the sett showed that it remained in use, for it probably contained more than one family, but the part from which Jess had emerged was not used by badgers for the rest of that summer. Any brothers and sisters she may have had would obviously have perished and probably remained unburied in one of the sett's chambers, a result of their mother's death.

3
A NEW FACE IN THE FAMILY

He took thee in his arms, and in pity brought thee home:
A blessed day for thee! then whither wouldst thou roam?
William Wordsworth

Jess soon settled completely into the general family routine. She was sleeping all night with the Bully, and sleeping for quite a lot of the day as well. When she was awake, however, she was very active, roaming the whole house and playing with anything that took her fancy. Though never as destructive as a puppy, she was particularly fond of brooms and shoes and greatly enjoyed pulling any curtains that came within her reach. Badgers are well known for their scrupulous cleanliness, both in themselves

and their domestic arrangements and, although we had provided Jess with an earth box in the pantry, it was used mainly for play and digging. Only twice during the whole time that she lived in the house did we have any sort of accident and that was before we finally learnt that whenever she asked to go out it was for a definite purpose, unlike a puppy, which will often be incontinent on first waking. Jess's natural badger instinct quickly led her to dig her own little latrine in a border conveniently close to the garden door where she could visit it regularly about three times a day.

Our dogs were always attracted by the heat of the Aga and boiler in the kitchen, against which they loved to lie and doze; Jess, too, soon discovered this delight but never realised, as they did, when it was unwise to be getting into the cook's way. Gill, for her part, naturally found cooking somewhat difficult with animals round her feet and for a time took to wearing gumboots, in case she accidentally stepped on the badger while trying to cope with her saucepans. Later, however, she cunningly devised a distraction by hanging a cork from a string attached to one side of the Aga rail which never failed to attract Jess if it was jerked up and down. It was not long before bedlam began to break out during mealtimes when we were all gathered in the kitchen. Jess had invented a game of her own: creeping unobserved under our round table where there was the prospect of endless fun with many pairs of feet and shoe-laces. This usually ended up with everyone getting kicked except the badger, so Jess was declared *persona non grata* at meals and was banished from the kitchen until the washing up had been done.

One evening, when I was reading a book comfortably in an armchair, Jess, having exhausted all other possibilities in the sitting-room, climbed on to my lap and went to sleep. Alas, the peace and quiet didn't last for long. As soon as she awoke again her restless nature led her to explore the cushion in the chair, then the inside of my jacket. For a while I suffered this assault upon my back, but when she started to dig out the lining of my sleeve I thought it better to slip off the jacket to avoid more serious damage. If only I could have had a camera ready as she emerged struggling from the cuff!

For a long time I had been in close touch with the Mammal Society's Badger Recorder for Sussex, for whom I had been providing information on the setts in our area for a countrywide badger census that the society was conducting. It therefore seemed sensible to seek his advice on rearing a cub. He had no experience himself, but at once put me in touch with someone who had rescued a great many and who was kind enough to send some useful information on suitable feeding with advice on the most appropriate steps that should be taken to return a badger successfully to the wild. Valuable as all this was, there were certain complications in our case since Jess had been so completely adopted by the Bully. We therefore decided that, in the early stages at least, we would have to be guided by events. Obviously Jess couldn't go back to the wild before she was at least six months old and able to fend and feed for herself. It was also essential that she should by then have developed at least some of the natural instincts that would help to make her more acceptable to strange badgers.

Another source of useful information on the food and

characteristics of badgers was Ernest Neal's book*. Briefly, badgers are not carnivorous but omnivorous and need to eat quite a lot of food to support their abundant energy. Their diet varies widely with the seasons, and can comprise almost anything from baby rabbit (no badger can usually catch a full-grown one), beetles and wasp grubs, to large quantities of earthworms, grass, nuts or other vegetation and roots. Although farmers and gamekeepers sometimes claim that badgers take eggs, or even kill poultry and game, I suspect that they are not normal in their diet and this will be the work of an old or exceptionally hungry animal at a time when food is hard to come by. Then, like any other animal that has acquired a particular habit, a badger will not readily give it up again.

In spring and autumn the badger's main source of food is found on permanent pastureland, over which they run at night, mainly searching for earthworms and succulent grass, and I have noticed that, should these pastures be ploughed, the neighbouring badgers sometimes transfer their homes and activities elsewhere. It has been said that a badger is willing and able to travel up to four miles in a night in its search of food. On the other hand, if food is plentiful in their vicinity, they will not normally go that far, and under normal circumstances do not go more than a mile from their setts. They are, however, very territorial by nature, and many of their instincts and habits are related to maintaining their individual territories, though this subject is still not yet fully understood. They also have strong clannish instincts: large numbers may often be found leading remarkably contented communal lives in the same sett, but they can be extremely aggressive towards the members of other clans at certain times of the year. This hostility is probably concerned with the food supply, but it may not be unconnected with their mating instincts. Very little has been

* Ernest Neal, *The Badger*, Collins, London (New Naturalist monograph).

recorded about the badger's territorial and social habits, presumably because of the difficulty in obtaining reliable and comprehensive evidence.

The farmland which surrounded our house and garden was often visited at night by badgers and this, we knew, would be our main difficulty when it came to returning Jess to the wild. The local badger population would almost certainly react with hostility to any stranger found trespassing on what they would regard as their own territory, particularly if she smelt of human beings and their dogs. That Jess would ultimately integrate with them was our hope, but how it could be achieved was something which we felt would have to be faced in due course. To have tried returning Jess to her own colony several miles away would, we thought, be altogether too difficult to supervise.

While the Bully continued to suckle Jess, we felt we had to treat her as we would a puppy. Supplementary feeding did not turn out to be the problem I had anticipated as she soon developed a wholesome appetite, and gladly ate whatever was going.

When suckling from the Bully, Jess was far gentler than any bull-terrier puppy we have had, who often scratched and pawed their mothers to ensure their share. Jess, of course, had no competition; but she would naturally wrap her tongue round the Bully's teats to suck, and never bit or scratched at her foster mother, even after she had grown quite a few sharp front teeth.

Throughout all this the Bully behaved magnificently and was remarkably tolerant of her restless little charge. It was a great pleasure to watch her playing with, and jealously guarding, her strange foster cub. She would allow Jess considerable latitude at times, but would always issue a severe correction whenever she thought the occasion demanded it. Once the badger's teeth grew sharper, the Bully would never suffer her ear's to be chewed, as she had when Jess was small.

A badger's musking habits must have seemed very

odd and unnatural to a bull-terrier. Like weasels, stoats, otters and other mustelids, badgers have musk glands at the root of their tails which they use to imprint their scent on other clan members and to mark strange territory at intervals when engaged on a journey of any length–presumably so that they can pick up the return trail. On familiar ground, the reasons for their musking are obscure and probably serve various purposes related to staking their territorial claims; the siting of latrines at strategic points in an area may also be intended to warn off other badgers. Young badgers, excited or at play, noticeably scent the air around them. Jess developed the musking habit quite early and would often musk the Bully as well as my shoes–I suppose she intended this to indicate that we formed part of her clan–and would also musk any other object to which she took a fancy. Luckily, their scent is by no means as unpleasant to human beings as is the odour of a fox, being not unlike the faint smell of stale sweat.

Once Jess had recovered from her lameness, the girls and I began taking her, with the Bully and Trottie, for quite long evening walks. To avoid arousing unwanted interest among the local badgers, we started most of those early outings by first going a short distance by car. Provided the Bully was with her in the car, the ride did not worry Jess in the least. In fact, it seemed as if she too sensed that it meant some fun and games. She soon became as eager to go as the dogs, but unlike them could not jump up into the boot, and so had to be lifted to prevent her scrabbling claws doing damage to the paintwork. When lifting her, we invariably picked Jess up by the scruff of the neck, as her mother would have done; this is by far the best method of handling any young animal. But, if she wanted to avoid being picked up, she would deliberately put her neck on the ground to make it as difficult as possible, though she never offered any other resistance and we never put her on a lead.

We often visited near-by forestry plantations, where I knew there were no badgers and little chance of meeting other people with their dogs. Jess obviously enjoyed these outings in the long summer evenings, and once in the woods would either amble happily after the dogs, if they did not go too far and too fast, or run close at my heel. I don't think this was in any way a compliment to me, since she would happily follow any other member of the family or anyone else who happened to be about, but, all the same, she very carefully stopped to musk the ground from time to time in case she might get lost.

As with other nocturnal animals, a badger's eyesight is not very good in strong light, and is almost certainly monochrome. Vision appears to play a relatively minor part in their lives as they depend mainly on scent and sound. Jess could not, for instance, see readily more than thirty feet or so, and seemed quite unable to distinguish a stationary object, unless it happened to be close by; though she could instantly pick out the slightest movement, even at a distance. I have noticed a similar facility in sock lambs, and have wondered whether this may be one of the reasons why sheep instinctively follow one another and why badger cubs enjoy chasing each other as they do. This may have been the reason why Jess would readily follow at the heels of anyone she knew to be friendly without any sort of training.

Jess had an obvious aversion to strong sunlight, and on a bright day was inclined either to bury her head or shield her eyes with her paws. Sometimes she would retreat to a dark and cosy corner, preferably up the stairs on the landing, or in one of the girl's bedrooms, where it was completely quiet. If this was not allowed, one of her favourite spots was among the dirty clothes in the laundry basket, from which she often had to turn out the cat to gain possession. Our neutered tom was able to stand his ground with the dogs, but he could never understand the badger. On one occasion, after he had swiped Jess hard in the face, he was amazed to find it had no effect whatever. It didn't even make the badger angry.

Once she was asleep Jess was not easily aroused, but when awake, her hearing was acute. Like all badgers, she had a remarkable facility for being able to distinguish an unusual sound from normal background or distant noise. When everyone was together in the kitchen, there was usually a fairly high noise level; this didn't worry Jess any more than it did the dogs, but should someone raise a voice or drop a plate, or if the telephone rang, she was instantly alert, looking in the relevant direction. This was quite different from the reactions of a fox cub I once reared, which would immediately panic and dive for cover in such circumstances. Unlike most animals, a badger's ears are directionally fixed, and so, to ascertain exactly where a noise is coming from, it has to move its head. This sometimes gave the impression that Jess was actually looking at us over a distance, when she was in fact only trying to locate the direction of a sound we had made.

Our motley collection of animals and birds was largely due to a strong instinct for farming which my wife had inherited. She also liked to have as many bedrooms in our rambling old house as possible occupied by young children. Over the years, we had had many children of different nationalities to stay, or children whose parents worked abroad so that they were unable to join them for the holidays. For a time during that particular summer, Gill happened to give a short holiday to several children connected with Riding for the Disabled, all of whom took a most profound interest in our little orphaned cub. One night, as Gill was putting one little boy with a particularly inquiring nature to bed, Jess burst into his room. She larked around for several minutes, as though conscious of a highly appreciative and delighted audience, when the little boy suddenly asked, 'Why do badgers have such funny striped faces?'

This floored Gill, who stalled by promising him the information at breakfast as she hustled the badger from the room before her antics became too extravagant.

As is well known, the colour markings of wild creatures have evolved to assist in the survival of their species and are not simply fanciful decoration. This coloration is mainly related to the environment in which the animal lives by providing either camouflage to deceive predatory enemies or as an aid to procreation; sometimes, as may be the case with badgers, it is designed as a sort of warning to would-be attackers, often from among other members of their own species.

In the dark, except for the black and white stripes on their faces and on the tips of their ears, badgers are practically indistinguishable from their surroundings. In daylight, however, the hair of their coats usually appears greyish silver, but is in fact tri-coloured, their chests and legs being covered with black hairs. They also have a fluffy whitish tail, some four or five inches long, which is normally trailed behind them, or held to one side if the animal is being chased. Presumably they do this to avoid having it bitten.

An angry, excited or nervous badger can make all the hair of its coat stand on end, just as dogs and cats, when roused, will raise their hackles. With their long coats extended in this way, they can seem to be twice their normal size. The badger's peculiar facial marking has long intrigued naturalists, many of whom think it has most likely to have evolved either as a warning or a means of recognition. Since badgers usually distinguish one another by their scent, and have no natural enemies except their own kind, it seems to me most probable that their distinctive facial coloration must be meant primarily to deter attack from other badgers. A badger which turns its striped face away invites attack in the rear—as Jess was to learn for herself in due course.

For well over a month, the Bully and Jess slept in the same basket in the kitchen. Then Priscilla, whose bedroom was overhead, was awoken in the middle of one night by a rumpus going on below. The time had obviously come when Jess and the Bully would have to be separated, at least during the night. Jess was then growing fast, and amusing as it was to have such a friendly little badger running wild about the house, we had to start thinking seriously about the difficult task that lay ahead of returning her to a more natural environment. It seemed essential she should be weaned as soon as possible, before she became either too much of a household pet or too fixed on either the Bully or myself. It also seemed important that we should start gradually introducing her to a more nocturnal routine so she could indulge in the normal activities of her species by the time she was five or six months old—which is the usual age when badger cubs become more or less independent of their mothers. This was going to be a formidable undertaking, and delay, we had been advised, might seriously prejudice our chances of achieving it with success.

the wisterianda

'Always eager for a romp'

would follow close to hedgerows'

'Out came a familiar little snout'

4
STARDOM

The BBC soon got to hear
And called for Jess to appear.
Odd Ode, with permission of Cyril Fletcher

The first thing that had to be decided in planning Jess's general education before giving her full freedom was, where she should live when weaned from the Bully? Our particular stretch of countryside consisted of farms with fairly extensive woodlands, which probably supported as many as ten or twelve badgers to the square mile and contained quite a number of very large setts that probably housed more than one family. I knew there were two such setts less than a mile from our house, and suspected it was their occupants who visited our immediate vicinity from time to time. It would obviously be most undesirable to risk Jess meeting any of them before she was more or less able to stand up for herself.

Nearly all large setts have been excavated throughout the centuries by the prodigious efforts of generations of badgers, who frequently alter the topography of the banks in which they are often found. It is very rare to find an entirely new sett; one that may appear comparatively new will often turn out to be a renovation of one long since disused, though badgers will sometimes enlarge a rabbit burrow to make a temporary shelter. Badgers move about quite a lot and like to have several alternative refuges available for use in emergencies or lying up. Regular occupation and breeding, however, usually takes place in a sett specially prepared for the purpose. Setts are often found on downland, but I had noticed that all the bigger ones in our area were seldom situated far from water, and were usually either in a hedgerow or at the edge of woodland. They thus had reasonable cover in the summer and were not too distant from their normal supplies of food. One only very rarely finds setts that are deep in the middle of large woods.

The number of entrances to a sett varies from time to time and only provides a rough guide to its size since much depends on natural causes, and whether or not the local hunt, or other people, have earthed them up. The labyrinth of interconnected tunnelling is often very extensive and deep and will frequently run under a stratum of sandstone or other rock, which help to keep the chambers dry.

Of the several small setts quite close to Old Farm Place, the nearest was in a wood only a quarter of a mile away; this had been extensively renovated the previous winter, but did not appear to be permanently in use. Even so, it was possible that it might be visited occasionally, and was obviously unsuitable for Jess. As she had come from quite a different colony, she would almost certainly have been regarded as a trespasser if found in occupation, which could have led to a vicious or even fatal attack. So, for the time being at any rate, it seemed that we would have to provide her with an artificial underground home of her own in an area she already knew.

Jess had clearly come to regard our garden as her territory, and roamed it fairly freely. So we decided this was, therefore, where her first sett must be. Towards the end of May, the Bully began to show the first signs of weaning Jess, and one weekend, when our youngest son, Andrew, was at home, we set to work and dug. The site we chose was at the bottom of the garden in a bank thickly covered with bracken and brambles, one side of which faced our adjoining field, where there was a small copse and pond. There we laboriously tunnelled some six feet from the back of the bank, where we prepared a covered position suitable for the large packing case that Jess was already using as a temporary refuge in the stable. I had read of artificial badger setts being made with nine-inch drain pipes, but pipes of that size are not easy to acquire, and, apart from their expense, the idea seemed to us to be altogether *too* artificial. So we decided to roof the entrances in the bank, which all led to our tunnel, with old sheets of corrugated iron, bent into an inverted U. These had been willingly donated by Basil Crisford, our kindly neighbour farmer. It proved an excellent and surprisingly easy method of construction and after comparatively few hours of labour we had a complete sett with some thirty feet of earth-floored tunnelling.

Badgers always give their setts more than one hole to provide a free flow of air, so we gave Jess the choice of three separate entrances. One was fairly obvious, but the other two were well concealed by a jungle of bracken, cow parsley and grass. These all led to a central chamber, from which the tunnel ran back under the bank to the box. We provided the box with special ventilation and, to make it more or less sound-proof, earthed it up to the lid which was hinged and covered with old roofing felt. It was agreed that the lid should never be opened while Jess was inside, so as not to disturb her sense of complete security when underground. Once the grass and bracken had regrown a few weeks later, it all looked a most professional job.

I had heard that badger sows will sometimes suckle their cubs for as long as five months. Jess, however, was only some four months old when the Bully stopped feeding her, and had by then moved naturally and easily on to solid food. First it was powdered milk with cereal three times a day, then puppy meal with a little meat and gravy, and finally it was on to ordinary dog food, liberally mixed with vegetables which she loved and often ate first. To vary their diet, our dogs were usually given fish once a week. This must have seemed most unusual to a badger, but Jess ate all we gave with equal relish and would even enjoy gnawing a bone. As with a dog, it always seemed to taste much better if carried to a dark secluded corner; she may, of course, have been taking precautions in case the dogs should try to take it from her, but she had no inclination, as they had, to put it in store for later use.

As soon as the Bully began to wean Jess, we started to separate them at nights, putting Jess in the stable around midnight so as to accustom her to the loss of the Bully's company. Following several nights of this rather strict detention, early one morning I introduced Jess to her artificial sett with the box in place at the rear of the bank. After a thorough inspection of the area, and of our navvying in particular, she went straight down and did not re-emerge until that evening. This seemed a most rewarding return on our efforts, and an encouraging sign that she approved of our idea of what a badger sett should be. Except for a couple of experimental days spent under a near-by woodshed, which she must have found both draughty and noisy, she accepted our sett as home during daylight hours from then on.

This happened to be the time when the BBC made brief television stars of Jess and the Bully.

We had tried to avoid too much publicity about the Bully's adoption of a badger, except among our immediate neighbours, but word gradually went around locally, mainly through Joanna's school friends, some of whom were often at the house to ride or swim. One day some friends came to tea, who, having lost their way, sought directions from a little girl standing rather forlornly by the roadside. She was, in fact, Priscilla's god-daughter and knew us very well but overcome by shyness, she stared blankly in reply to their questions until casually asked whether she happened to know where the badger lived. At once Martha's eyes lit up, and she gave them accurate and clear instruction.

The story obviously had an appeal for children, so we were eventually persuaded to approach BBC Television. A friend had suggested that the 'Blue Peter' programme might be the most suitable, so I rang one of the producers to ask whether they would be interested in a story about a badger cub that was being reared by a bitch.

'But of course,' came the unhesitating reply. 'It would make a very suitable programme. Please bring them along to our studio.'

BBC producers are obviously making difficult engagements on the phone all day long, and I pictured someone accustomed only to clap his hands for everything to fall into place. For my part, I was appalled at the thought of having to take a reluctant bull-terrier, still cumbersome with milk, with a wriggling half-grown badger up to London, whether by car or by train, so stuttered my apologies and said that would be quite impossible. The two animals would certainly never co-operate in a studio atmosphere, and the last thing I wanted was to give a lot of viewers the idea that badger cubs make suitable and easily transportable pets.

'I'm afraid,' I said, 'that neither of them are circus-trained and we have no special tricks. It's just a simple little story of a bitch fostering a badger cub, which we hope to return to the wild in due course.' I began to have visions of hoards of people asking to come and see them for themselves. 'If you want the story for "Blue Peter",' I went on, 'I'm afraid you'll have to bring your circus to us.'

There was a pause in the conversation. The silence was punctuated by what sounded like fingers snapping with annoyance at this frustration to instant decision-making. He may, of course, have been flicking over the pages of his diary, but, whatever the cause of the noises-off, I was by that stage fully expecting the proposal to be turned down.

'All right,' he said suddenly, 'what about next Wednesday? If you could ring me again tomorrow, I'll have worked out the details.'

Most of that evening was spent trying to plan the things that might make an interesting television appearance, and I began by jotting down a few notes which eventually ran into several pages of foolscap. Our telephone call the next day lasted less than thirty seconds.

'We'll travel down by train tomorrow afternoon and will meet you by the ticket barrier at Charing Cross,' said the producer. 'You'll recognize us. We're all good-looking.'

'But what about the cameras . . . ?' I began to stutter.

'They'll come by road.'

'But . . .'

'It'll be all right. There's nothing you need to worry about.'

All it seemed that I had to do was to arrange next day to take a half-day off, and that was that. Everything was settled and amateurs like me clearly didn't need to know any details and might as well relax.

This did not, of course, appeal to Gill, who at once began to cross-question me that evening. How many would there be? Would they want a meal? Where were they going to film the action? How long would it take?

'We'll have to play it off the cuff,' was the only advice I could offer. Further telephone calls to the producer would simply get us nowhere. In any case, wasn't she used to instant catering for hoards of children and well schooled in their impromptu entertainment?

'All right,' Gill said, 'but *I'm* not taking part in it, and if they want to bring Jess into my kitchen they must put up with me in gumboots. I'm not having my ankles nipped just to amuse the BBC.'

Priscilla and Joanna were most excited at the thought that they were going to meet real live TV personalities, and Lesley Judd in particular. She, they said, was one of the presenters of this popular children's programme, all of whom seemed to be household names. Lesley, I was given to understand, had all the charm necessary to bring out the best in the most unpredictable animals, including badgers.

The next morning I went up to London as usual and made my way back to Charing Cross at the appointed hour, only to find that television people are as indistinguishable as anyone else in a crowd. There was no Blue Peter flag, which, as a sailor, I should instantly have recognized, and there were a great many good-looking people around. Just as I was beginning to think that our arrangements had gone astray, I was approached by a perfectly ordinary young man who had somehow instantly recognized me. With him was an attractive young girl whom I assumed to be Lesley Judd, but who, after a hurried introduction, turned out to be an associate producer. I asked what had happened to Miss Judd.

'Teeth,' muttered the producer as we ran down the platform to find an empty carriage before the signal turned to green. It seemed he was not going to be much more explicit off the telephone than he had been on it, and just as I was assuming that I would be left to puzzle it all out for myself, his colleague came to my rescue.

'He means wisdom teeth,' she said. 'She's just had two of them out and can neither talk nor smile. We'll take all the shots we can today and come back with her in a few days' time.'

Unfortunately the train was quite full, and we had to share a compartment with two other passengers whose ears pricked up visibly when my companions began cross-questioning me intensely even before it had started to move. I am not one of those people who enjoy chattering in trains and I somewhat hesitatingly proffered my laboriously assembled notes of what might make an interesting programme. These were quickly and politely scanned – and laid aside. Instead, the two producers continued to quiz me about Jess and the Bully and badgers in general while they made copious notes of their own. 'They most likely couldn't read your writing,' suggested Gill when we talked things over at the end of the day.

Throughout all this our two fellow-travellers sat fascinated as the whole story unfolded on the way to Tonbridge, where they thanked us profusely as the train drew into the station.

'It's been such a delightful journey,' they said, opening the door. 'We only wish we could come all the way with you to see the filming. We do hope it goes all right and we will see it later on TV.'

As we drove up from the station we met the Blue Peter convoy in a miracle of timing, and so arrived all together at Old Farm Place. As soon as the equipment had been unloaded we trooped through the house into the garden, where we found Gill and the girls exchanging local gossip with Annette Bowman, the wife of our nearest farmer neighbour. When they heard that Lesley Judd was not among the visitors, Priscilla and Joanna at once voiced their general disappointment.

'What, no actress?' said Annette, who had gained some experience in amateur theatricals in our village hall. 'Let me fill the role.'

The Producer muttered something about contracts and Equity, and eyed her in much the same way as he had eyed and discarded my notes.

'No,' he said firmly, 'we must have Lesley for this job, even though it will mean another visit. She's excellent with animals.'

Rustic folk like us may have acting talent in their midst, but we were obviously out of our depth when it came to handling animals, unions or contracts. Meanwhile Gill's face fell visibly at the prospect of yet another invasion.

'Anyway,' continued the producer, as we rounded up the Bully and Jess, 'let's get down to work and take all the film we can in case the bull-terrier weans the badger in the meantime, as I understand she may.'

They therefore concentrated on getting a lot of film of

the Bully suckling Jess and made a lot more notes on how they thought the story should be presented.

A week later a similar but different party arrived; happily with a smiling Lesley Judd, and we went through the whole performance once again. By then the producers had prepared a detailed script, which they were anxious to keep to as closely as possible. Fortunately the Bully was still suckling Jess, who was by then spending her days in the garden sett. It was a lovely sunny afternoon, but, television or no television, I was anxious not to wake Jess up too early because of her dislike of strong sunlight. On the other hand, that was what the cameramen wanted, and there was a lot of talk about having to pay the technicians overtime, so I was none too popular for refusing to allow her to be woken before six o'clock. However, we all felt much more at ease than we had done the week before–familiarity was beginning to breed confidence, and Gill had provided a sumptuous tea to pass the time. This went a long way to restoring morale and, judging by the way in which they did justice to Gill's scones, we thought the BBC must keep their employees on very short rations.

As evening approached we all trooped off down the garden and summoned the Bully, who was busy about other things, to go and wake Jess. Meanwhile Lesley Judd and I stood some way off so that the cameramen could take some delightful shots as the two animals greeted each other nose to nose at the entrance to the sett. As soon as Jess had grown used to the sunlight, Lesley and I were filmed handling her and talking badgers in an impromptu sort of way. She was very sensibly clad in country clothes and was clearly used to handling unfamiliar young animals. Jess's paws were, however, very muddy at the time and although she had wiped most of it off on to my jacket, I was somewhat disconcerted to see a large brown streak all down Lesley's cheek as Jess quickly hid her head in her hair. It all made a charming little scene but, as we made our way back to the house, closely followed by a platoon of men with cameras and microphones picking up our every word, Lesley hurriedly handed Jess back to me, saying–unscripted–'You know, this badger bites.' And so she could, for she then proceeded to demolish the rose I had put in my buttonhole to grace the occasion, before starting on my arm and sleeve.

Our kitchen was by then crammed with people, equipment and flood-lighting, but despite this overcrowded atmosphere in their familiar surroundings, the Bully willingly obliged by allowing Jess to suckle. Lesley and I meanwhile played our scripted parts, these mainly comprising a series of questions and answers–with a few wisecracks about badgers thrown in for good measure. All went surprisingly well, and I found working to a script with a professional actress was as relaxing as an informal conversation with royalty. The Bully and Jess were then filmed feeding from their respective bowls, and we all trooped back into the garden, now looking its best in the late evening light.

Almost immediately things began to grow rather hectic. The principal stars, no doubt sensing they had a large and highly professional audience, began to let their hair down and started to rag violently about, like children at a party after they've had their tea. The producers, accustomed to actors doing just as they are told, became frantic, and I was deluged with appeals to restore order, despite my warning that nothing could be guaranteed. Their carefully prepared script might just as well have been thrown to the wind. They were clearly unprepared for the scene that followed: a badger and a bull terrier were rushing madly around the lawn, in and out of groups of people and between their legs. It was all too close and fast-moving for the cameramen, who had obviously had little experience of filming animals around their feet. One of them dropped his splendid camera in an effort to find a focus, while his colleagues, the sound recorders, just stood back and laughed. Eventually everyone gave up. The producers suggested that Lesley and I should take Jess for

a walk, without the bouncing Bully, across the field below the house which was still bathed in sunlight. By then Lesley had got the measure of her co-star and, after the cameras had been posted at strategic points, she set off with Jess following obligingly at her heel. It all looked an excellent performance and we, watching from a distance, were thankful that it didn't occur to our friendly old sheep or the ponies to try and join in.

As soon as all this was done, and no doubt still thinking of their budget, the producers were anxious to be off. But the crew, perhaps with overtime in mind, seemed in no hurry to depart and stayed chatting happily with us for a while. When they finally prepared to drive away, a good-humoured cameraman held up a length of film to the sunset saying jokingly: 'It all looks jolly good to me.'

The 'Blue Peter' programme is normally broadcast live, and, fearing it might bring an influx of local visitors all hoping to see Jess for themselves, we asked them not to put it out until later in the year when we hoped she might have been successfully returned to the wild. When we saw the film eventually, it made a delightful and charming little item, but to us, who had been so involved in its production, it naturally seemed to be much too short.

So the story was recorded and seen by millions, but the main actors showed no signs of exhaustion or that sudden stardom had gone to their heads. Life for them went on as usual, but Gill and I were delighted it had gone off more or less as we had hoped.

5
ALARMS IN THE NIGHT

But what they fought each other for
I could not well make out.
Robert Southey

One unforeseen difficulty that came up soon after Jess took up daily residence in her artificial sett was that the dogs, particularly Trottie, who could get down it easily, would wake her whenever they felt inclined. This had to be stopped, but we still allowed them to give her a call at about 6 p.m. After she had sleepily emerged and become accustomed to the light, Jess would carefully carry out her grooming ritual before visiting a lavatory she had conveniently established close by among the bracken. This done, she usually either shambled off around the garden on her own, or had a game with the dogs before eventually turning up in the house for her food.

Once I had had my own supper I would, whenever possible, take them all off for a walk and when we got back Jess was given the full run of the house and garden until midnight. We then gave her another meal before confining her to the stable, where she was well provided with playthings, until morning. Although, so far as we knew, Jess felt no inclination to wander from the familiar territory of the garden, it seemed unwise to risk her going too soon on to ground where she might encounter other badgers. I suspected that she spent at least some of those early nights trying to scratch her way out of the stable, but the door had been sheathed with tin, to save both it and her claws from damage. She was always fast asleep, in a cosy little nest of straw underneath the manger, when I went out early in the morning with her breakfast, which was often scorned in her anxiety to get back down her sett.

It was obviously wrong to keep a young growing badger captive during the hours when she would normally be most active in searching for food, and so, after about fourteen nights of this rather strict detention, I felt that the moment had arrived when she must be given all-night leave. To try to discourage her from straying, we secretly left her midnight meal where she could find it for herself and then awaited events with some trepidation.

For several nights nothing happened. Jess clearly never left the garden. There was often evidence next day to show that she had passed at least some of the night digging in odd places and generally playing around the house. Once we found a dead but uneaten mole; some pansies and wallflowers that Gill had carefully planted and nursed in a border were several times uprooted; little holes appeared here and there in the lawn, where, presumably, she had searched out earthworms which rarely come to the surface at that time of the year. There was, however, never any damage which could not easily be repaired, and at least it showed that she was beginning to feel quite at home in the dark.

The domestically acquired habit that Jess was most reluctant to forego was her nightly encounter with the Bully when she was put out for her 'late-night final'.

They were always eager for a romp, despite the inequality in size and weight, but Jess would instinctively use her head and body like a battering-ram and was always careful to keep her nose well away from trouble. It has been said that hitting a badger on the head is quite useless, for it will simply shake it and shamble off. But a badger's nose is quite a different matter; it is by far their most sensitive organ, and, unlike that of a dog, protrudes some way beyond the skull and jaw. Jess took great care that her stubby snout was never bitten in those mock battles, though, given half a chance, she would never hesitate to take a quick nip at the Bully's tail and legs. The Bully, for her part, always tried to grab Jess by the scruff of the neck or to bowl her over. Sometimes it looked rather rough stuff, but we rarely interfered so long as it remained natural, good-hearted play.

Jess's judo-like tactic of a headlong charge, followed by a split-second broadside tackle to knock the opponent's legs from under her, worked very well with a Jack Russell like Trottie, but a bull-terrier was far too heavy and sturdy in the legs for this technique to have any hope of success, though it was not for want of trying. This original manoeuvre made me wonder whether it was the instinctive method by which a badger deals with a fox; for foxes are definitely chary of antagonizing them. It was obviously such a simple and effective way of toppling a taller animal while keeping the sensitive nose well away from trouble. When two badgers fight, the challenger's opening gambit is presumably a similar kind of charge, before it develops into a barging and biting match until one or the other turns tail and runs.

Jess had a well-developed sense of curiosity that would sometimes amount to impudence. If we kept her out of the house in the evening, she would invariably make repeated attempts to get indoors to see what was going in the way of entertainment. Her ideas of entertainment were not always ours. She would scratch violently at each of our four outside doors in turn, two of which open outwards–and even these should could open with her claws unless they were firmly latched. Being kept outside infuriated Jess at first and made her scratch and rattle all the harder, but, as time went on, her badgering of a door, as we used to call it, became little more than a greeting, as though to say, 'I'm here. Can I please come in?' and she

soon learnt to look elsewhere for amusement when no answer was forthcoming.

Ever since she was a child Gill had kept bantams of one sort or another, and at the time when Jess was with us she had three different breeds: Polish, Silkies and Pekins, all of whom were rearing families in their own special runs in odd corners of the garden. Most of their coops had been knocked together out of old tea-chests, or anything that had come to hand, and in addition had very makeshift shutting up arrangements which were optimistically thought by Gill to be fox-proof. Our local foxes must have been extremely cowardly or unintelligent creatures, for her security was very elementary: she often relied on odd bits of wood or old trays with a maze of tangled wire netting anchored here and there by odd bricks. While all this might be adequate for foxes, it stupidly never occurred to me that these rudimentary precautions might not in fact be badger-proof.

One night, soon after Jess had been given all-night leave, Gill and I were sharply woken at two o'clock in the morning by a resounding crash, quite close to the house. This was quickly followed by hysterical squawking and realizing at once what must have happened, we slipped out of bed. After frantically searching for a torch, we rushed to the scene, anticipating disaster. There, as we expected, was a tea-chest, supposed to be accommodating a Pekin cock and hen with twelve little chicks, lying sadly on its side. Alas, the cock lay dead outside his house: true to his breed, he had obviously tried to defend his young family and been nipped in the neck for his valour. There was Jess, doing her best to goad the hen to play, while the unfortunate bird clucked madly for her chicks who were scattered in all directions.

There had been no malice; the hutch had simply got in her way as she explored that part of the garden. She was quite unmoved by our sudden and noisy arrival. She probably thought it something of an unexpected bonus, and raised no objection to being hastily removed from the scene. So it ended up with her having to spend the rest of that night alone in the stable where there would be no further amusement. Though Gill conceded that it had been an accident and that the attack had not been premeditated, it was several days before she forgave Jess, or me, for the loss of her best Pekin cock.

Meanwhile something had to be done to reorganize Gill's improvized bantam housing and make it more or less proof against badgers. The obvious solution was to go back to medieval principles and concentrate all her poultry within some kind of stockade. This is what was done, with the result that from then on we had a shanty-town of packing-cases enclosed in a flimsy wire screen with only one gateway in one corner of the garden. Unfortunately, the roots of trees prevented us from digging the netting firmly into the ground, so its security was still rather illusory, but all the same Jess never tried to dig her way into the enclosure.

Shutting the bantams up at dusk was, however, quite another matter and became something of an art to do it before Jess could offer her assistance, as she invariably did if she happened to be about. Once, unbeknown to Gill, Jess actually managed to get herself shut inside the stockade. Before long agitated bantam sounds made themselves heard even in the house, disturbing what should have been the quietness and peace of evening. Luckily for me, perhaps, I was not at home. With the earlier incident fresh in mind, Gill rushed out in no mood for soft words, but when she arrived on the scene, anger was reduced to laughter. There, looking cheekily at her from the door of a hutch, was the face of a badger, behind whom were two completely unharmed but highly agitated Silkie hens. Here was proof, if it was needed, that well-fed young badger cubs at least do not normally kill chickens for fun as a fox cub will. If they were driven by hunger in other circumstances, however, I imagine it could be quite a different story.

It may be thought that we seldom had a good night's sleep that summer, and I must admit that in the early days of Jess's night-time freedom I was often subconsciously alert, particularly when a car was heard going down the lane late at night. We also knew that sooner or later she would have to meet our local badgers, and early in July Gill and I were woken in the middle of the night by a far more alarming noise than any we had heard up till then. It was one which I had long expected and feared. Excited badger cries began to rend the still night air, as, on the lawn immediately beneath our bedroom window, a serious badger fight broke out. Tumbling out of bed, dazed with sleep, snatching only slippers and the strong torch that I by then always kept handy, we rushed downstairs and roused a reluctant Bully, who was as usual at such an hour deep in her own private dreamland and oblivious to the danger facing her cub. With much clamour and shout-

ing we sallied forth into the darkness, only to find that the fight had moved out of the garden, across the lane and into the adjacent field and, by the sound of it, was rapidly going downhill into the valley.

We were hardly appropriately clad for a cross-country steeple-chase. Gill was wearing a flimsy summer night-dress and I my thinnest Hong Kong pyjamas. But the fight appeared a life-and-death affair and the fate of a very special member of our family was undoubtedly in the balance. We stumbled down the bank, across the lane and clambered over the near-by gate, which was of the Sussex slide-bar type and much too clumsy to draw in a hurry. The field was occupied by the girls' ponies and our former sock lamb, Rebecca, who was by then three years old and of mammoth proportions. She had never accepted the fact that she had grown up and become a sheep, and considered herself the equal of all the human members of our family. She always slept close by the gate, so as to be near the house, and was quite unmoved by all the noise. She obviously thought our sudden appearance was for her sole benefit. 'Food,' she was probably saying to herself, 'and at this time of night. What a very kindly thought,' and, taking full advantage of Gill's lack of mobility in bedroom slippers, soon had her effectively pinned against the hedge. To corner more than one of us at a time was, however, quite beyond her, so leaving Gill to talk her way out of the confrontation as best she could, I ran painfully on through the knee-high thistles shouting at the top of my voice. The Bully, by then in full possession of her wits, had roared off into the darkness, snorting angrily as she went, and I was tempted, for a moment, to leave all the heroics to her. A bull-terrier on the warpath is, after all, a formidable opponent for any adversary.

After what seemed like an interminable period of suspense, in which I could only guess at the direction the combatants had taken, there was an agonizing badger scream from the direction of the bog at the bottom of the hill. In dismay I felt that it could only mean one thing: that the stranger had sunk its teeth deep into Jess. Then all went ominously silent, except for the sound of the Bully, who seemed to be doing some sort of military encircling act, crashing around on the far side of the valley, among scrub and brambles where I dared not venture. Uppermost in my mind was an image of Jess lying somewhere in the bog, injured or even worse. Badgers have been known to fight to the death and I was desperate for some sort of clue. I called her again by name and raked the whole length of the valley with the strong beam of my torch. By then Gill had managed to extricate herself from her predicament and had caught me up; with the sheep, of course, as her *aide-de-camp*.

At first my anguished calls for Jess received no response: then there was a rustling in the reeds below us and suddenly a familiar black-and-white striped face came struggling out of the bog. Jess shambled happily to my feet. She had undoubtedly been the victor not the vanquished and, although rather wet and grimey from the site where she had delivered her decisive *coup de grâce,* she was otherwise quite unharmed. If Rebecca's thought had centred on the possibility of a midnight feast, it was equally easy to read Jess's as she grunted up the hill: 'That saw the dirty beggar off.' Even the grin on her face might have been discernible.

Greatly relieved by such a happy ending to her first encounter with a wild badger, Gill and I threaded our way carefully back through the thistles to the gate, with Rebecca and Jess close upon our heels. Once we had reached the security of her own territory, we left Jess in the garden for the rest of the night and returned thankfully to bed. For the first time in weeks we slept soundly for the rest of the night, confident that Jess was well able to look after herself and was growing up just like any other badger, despite her somewhat unnatural upbringing.

It seemed likely, on reflection, that the intruder was probably a full-grown badger, since a young cub would have been most unlikely to have come that far alone. It must therefore have been Jess who had made most of the excited noises which had woken us so abruptly. Might it have been a call for help, we wondered? Perhaps it was her idea of demonstrating her ownership of our garden and her reluctance to share it with another badger; or she might, of course, have thought that we poor sleepy humans needed her special protention.

The next evening I deliberately took Jess for a walk across the battlefield of the night before and was glad to notice how she was much more relaxed than usual, being quite prepared to leave me to go snuffling about on her own. She may even have been looking for another adversary, for, after all, it was now her own territory by right of conquest.

The successful outcome of this chance encounter prompted me to extend Jess's knowledge of our immediate neighbourhood rather sooner than I had originally intended. She was then not five months old, and would in the wild have still been dependent on her parent for instruction and protection. Thanks to the circumstances of her early life and her subsequent fostering by the Bully, Jess was, without a doubt, developing the most important natural characteristics of a badger in driving off unwanted visitors to its own home ground. It might be thought that, since badgers do lead gregarious lives, a solitary little cub would have welcomed the arrival of another member of its own species. On the contrary, they are a very tribal lot, and Jess probably considered it her duty to see that we, as members of her family, were valiantly defended against all strangers.

Slowly but surely Jess was growing less dependent on the Bully; force of circumstances had already deprived her of the company of Trottie, who by then had a young family of her own. Although I maintained that there would be no harm done, Gill was particularly concerned to ensure that Jess and Trottie's pups never met for fear of what might follow; so her arrival at the house in the evening would be heralded by cries of warning, and it was the duty of the first person to see her coming to slam all the doors. But just as Jess's former roistering with Trottie had to be outlawed for the time being, so her interest began to develop in other directions. One of her favourite pastimes was to turn out the summer house, which had no door and was invariably full of interesting playthings: cushions, chairs, a lilo, rugs and croquet balls were all fair game, and by morning the place usually looked as though a typhoon had passed that way.

At the time when Trottie had become temporarily *hors de combat*, the Bully began to assume an air of not wanting to know Jess when she was in the house, and any attempt by the badger to get into her bed would be fiercely repulsed–particularly if it concealed a bone. As long as things didn't get too rough, we felt that this provided a salutory lesson to the effect that dogs could also get savage when they wanted to be. We therefore rarely interfered, but left it to those concerned to sort matters out for themselves. Jess usually took the hint and was all the more ready to accompany me alone for walks, so I found myself gradually assuming the role of a foster-father.

My evening walks with Jess usually began when it was still daylight. We would follow close to hedgerows and go through the woods, or anywhere there was a little cover. Instinct, or her late mother's influence, had already taught Jess that open ground was strictly for use only after dark, and she gradually grew more and more willing to leave me and go rootling off on her own, only returning now and then to make sure she had not been abandoned. While she was obviously finding certain things to eat, it was often impossible to see what they were. She definitely consumed a certain amount of grass, and on one occasion I noticed she tackled a glow-worm, which gleamed from her mouth like a miniature torch for some time until I think she decided it was better left alone.

Despite the loss of her best bantam cock, and frequent but usually mock attacks on her ankles, Gill was slowly coming to regard Jess with great favour and to accept her as one of the family. One of Gill's great interests, apart from her livestock and the activities of visiting children, was in her flowers and her rock garden. The latter usually suffered severely from the predations of slugs and snails, but once a badger's main territory includes your garden, these pests soon cease to be a serious menace.

For Jess, slugs were real delicacies, though she appeared to have a strong dislike of their slime and it was interesting to see how she dealt with this particular problem. She would carefully roll them with a paw on grass or a stone until the wetness was removed before consuming them with obvious relish. She only played with snails at first, and had to be shown how their shells could be broken before the tasty part was revealed. People who complain that badgers do damage in their gardens by digging for earthworms and other things, may overlook the good they do in keeping the slug and snail populations in check. So far as we were concerned, the benefits far outweighed any damage suffered by the lawns or borders, and though she loved lettuce and cooked vegetables (but not fruit) in her food, Jess never took any interest whatever in the kitchen garden and did not interfere with its contents in any way.

At the end of one particularly hot and trying day that

summer, Gill decided to restore her nerves to normal by taking the dogs for a walk in the hope of seeing some interesting wildlife. It was not often that she managed to escape from the family for a quiet stroll. At dusk, in summer, the surrounding countryside can be wonderfully peaceful, and she especially wanted to see if the nightingales had returned to a particular spinney. It would, of course, have been much better to have gone without the dogs: with them crashing around there was really little hope of seeing much, let alone of hearing a nightingale sing.

Down the lane, through a wood, across a field she went and on into a little copse where there was a pond in what had been, in medieval times, one of the old iron quarries for which, with their associated furnaces and hammer ponds, our part of Sussex was famous. No sooner had Gill arrived near the pond than she heard a puffing and blowing from behind. It seemed quite unrelated to the dogs, and turning she saw a familiar white-striped face, galloping triumphantly towards her in the twilight. Obviously Jess had been upset at not being included in the walk and had followed up their scent. She madly capered several times round Gill in ever-decreasing circles, finally bumping heavily against her legs. As she had never before been for a walk with Jess in the evening, Gill didn't realize that this was one of her ideas of a friendly little greeting. Equal delight was also shown towards the dogs, but as they were busy about their own affairs they didn't seem to share the badger's enthusiasm. In fact, Trottie, who was by then somewhat wary of vigorous play with Jess, managed to keep her distance by running round in ever-widening circles. Eventually these mad gyrations exhausted them all, and with a sigh Gill resigned herself to the fact that this really was the only wildlife she was likely to come across that night.

Starting for home, across the field and through the narrow path bordered by brambles in the wood, they formed a procession. Trottie wisely took up station ahead to get some protection from Jess who was following astern, stopping every now and then to investigate the undergrowth or eat a beetle. She always caught up again with a rush and a bump against Gill's heels. Becoming thoroughly unnerved at this sort of treatment, Gill then coaxed Jess to walk in front so that Trottie had to suffer all the rushes and bumps. Finding this even less enjoyable, Trottie then turned on Jess in anger and, to ensure some peace and order on the march, Gill then picked up and carried Trottie (preferring her to Jess). For a while all went well, but even a Jack Russell is no mean weight to carry over a distance and, besides this, Gill had to keep on stopping to avoid tripping over Jess, who once again began to fall behind: whereupon Gill decided the only thing to do was to make a quick dash for home.

Anyone who thinks badgers are slow and ponderous animals should try giving one the slip in a wood. Encumbered by the weight of Trottie, Gill soon realized that she was not nearly swift enough. Jess naturally thought it was some new kind of game, and managed a specially fast rush from behind that propelled her neatly between Gill's legs. She then stopped abruptly, to examine something in the path; Gill, of course, tripped and fell, and only a miracle prevented her from landing right on top of Jess. This sent Trottie sprawling into the brambles, where she promptly disappeared. Picking herself up, fortunately unhurt, and thankful that the badger had done no more than fluff up her coat at seeing such strange and alarming behaviour in a human, Gill managed to reach the bottom of the wood without further incident.

The dogs then reappeared as if from nowhere, and the procession re-formed for the long walk up a field towards our house. They were all on familiar ground again and Gill was at last beginning to enjoy her walk, but the pleasure was to be short-lived. Suddenly a bulky figure loomed ahead, silhouetted against the rising moon and firmly barring the way. It was, of course, Rebecca, who naturally claimed attention and took her place in the procession. Gill knew from bitter experience, it was most unwise to have a sheep who had a regrettable tendency to butt one behind the knees bringing up the rear. It was probably only misplaced affection, combined with a determination to have the pleasure of your company in the field. That evening Rebecca was particularly affectionate and determined and it took Gill a very long time to reach the safety of the gate. Her other companions, bored at the slow pace of the convoy, had romped on ahead, so Gill had to finish her walk alone walking backwards with one hand on a woolly head while she alternatively threatened and cajoled a cantankerous old sheep. When she did arrive home, hot and exhausted, she ran into a barrage of questions and comments:

'Where *have* you been?'

'We thought you must have got lost!'

'The dogs and Jess have been back for *ages.*'

'Did you have a nice peaceful walk?' was all I asked and, funnily enough, for once she had no breath with which to reply.

It was a long while before we learnt the whole story of her happy little stroll in the summer evening twilight with the dogs.

6
FRIENDS AND NEIGHBOURS

O wad some Pow'r the giftie gie us
To see oursels as others see us!
Robert Burns

Our fields beyond the garden adjoined three neighbouring farms. On the one side, and closest to the house, we had that of Mike Bowman, and on the other that of Basil Crisford. In between there was some woodland that belonged to three sisters who owned the third farm. Once Jess had her complete freedom, we realized, they could all in one way or another become involved when she began to establish a territory of her own. As soon as she was old enough, it therefore seemed a diplomatic move to introduce Jess to our long-suffering farming neighbours.

Most of them were already aware of my enthusiasm for badgers, about which Annette Bowman in particular had always been candid and outspoken. 'Why on earth,' rumour had reported she was wondering, 'should a grown-up man want to keep a badger?'

'Don't you think it would be much more interesting,' she said to Gill one day, 'if he kept a mistress instead?'

Her husband Mike was very keen on shooting, and I knew he viewed all badgers with a certain amount of distrust. One of my first tasks would therefore have to be to win Annette over to my cause, so one evening I took Jess over to their farm where we were duly invited into the sitting room. Annette had never seen a badger close to before and was clearly apprehensive when Jess started wandering all over the house. Since she had had considerable experience in rearing puppies and other animals, I found this rather peculiar and could only think she was expecting Jess to spend a penny on the sofa there and then. She was, however, most surprised to see such an immaculate fur coat and to find out how attractive and cuddly a little badger can be. But Mike, who came in later, was obviously less easily convinced; he had met a lot of badgers in his time and knew all about their teeth.

This formal introduction safely over, I felt we had gained at least one ally, but had overlooked the fact that Annette often let a cottage on their farm to summer visitors. That year a family called the Linns, who had come from New Zealand, happened to be spending their holidays on the farm, and one evening, when they were all in the sitting-room playing cards, there came what sounded like a knock at the door.

'It must be Annette with the eggs,' said Peggy Linn to one of her three children. 'Go and let her in, Michael.'

Michael did as he was bidden and left to answer the door, but there were no voices, only silence, until he called in astonishment: 'Crikey, Mum, come and have a look at this. It's like *The Wind in the Willows.*'

Whereupon Peggy Linn ran to the door and to her amazement there was a sleek and beautiful badger waiting on the step.

'Good evening, Mr Badger,' she said, picking up Michael's allusion with commendable presence of mind. 'Won't you please come in?'

Intrigued at the sound of this peculiar conversation, the rest of the family rushed to see what was happening and were equally amazed. There was the first real live badger they had ever seen and such things only happened in fairy tales or dreams. They stood around the door as the little badger, who needed no second bidding, calmly sauntered inside. Perturbed at what might happen next, Jane, their daughter, hastily climbed on to a chest of drawers to be out of harm's way, though she soon jumped down once she realized the animal was really friendly.

Leaving the badger to wander round the room, Peggy went into the kitchen and produced a saucer of milk. This was offered, with a little grated cheese, and immediately consumed by Jess, who allowed herself to be stroked like a puppy and proceeded to make herself quite at home. The family were naturally thrilled at having such an improbable visitor, but after about half an hour, during which time the badger had thoroughly explored the cottage, Peggy thought that the visit had gone on long enough. Her offer of an open door was duly accepted, and the badger stole happily back into the night, without, I believe, making any gesture of thanks.

It was only by chance that I heard of this little escapade and hastened to explain the situation to the family, fearing that this sort of casual hospitality might undermine endeavours to return Jess to the wild. It turned out to be quite unnecessary, as the Linns were most understanding.

The Linns promised their co-operation in not encouraging or feeding her should she ever come back. In fact she never did visit them in the cottage again, but one night some weeks later, when they were camping in a field on the farm, Peggy awoke in the small hours to find something heavy on her bed. Feeling fur and reaching for a torch, she wasn't altogether surprised to discover the friendly little badger curled up fast asleep. It is hard to imagine how a camper who hadn't met a badger before might have reacted, but Peggy, not wishing to rouse the rest of her family, who were still fast asleep, thought it best to let sleeping badgers lie. However, Jess didn't stay very long, and there was a slight family eruption when she couldn't find the exit from the tent. The next night the same thing happened but on that occasion Jess did her best to dig herself inside Jane's sleeping-bag, and rather more persuasion was needed to make it quite clear that the family really preferred not to be badgered in the middle of the night.

As a family we too had always been great camping enthusiasts, and that summer, when the holidays came, Joanna carried on the family tradition.. With a French friend, Gabrielle Cottin, who was spending the summer with us, and three school friends, Lucy Theiss, Carol Saunders and Vivienne Cole, she also set up camp in a field not far away. It was a very well-organized affair as three of them were keen Girl Guides. Sometimes we could hear from the house the laughter and chatter around the camp fire before silence and tranquility descended as the girls retired to their tent for the night. Alas, they had paid little attention to my warning that too much noise from them might prove irresistible to Jess. And so it did. One night, as they were chattering sleepily in the tent by the light of a hurricane lamp, a crashing sound was heard in the dry undergrowth near by, followed by some scratching on the canvas of the tent whereupon there were shrieks of alarm from several of the inmates, who at first thought they were being invaded by the ponies or Rebecca. Gabrielle, Carol and Vivienne ducked their heads in panic into the safety of their sleeping-bags, but Lucy and Joanna heard some panting and realized it was probably only Jess.

Their supposition was soon confirmed when a little black nose was pushed under the side of the tent by Joanna's bed. Jess was, of course, delighted at finding such promising company. Lucy and Joanna were reduced to helpless giggles, whereupon other curious heads began to emerge from cover, but the sight of a disembodied if eager wet nose struck them with terror once again, and total pandemonium broke out in the camp. In an effort to restore calm, Joanna grabbed her hairbrush–the only available weapon she could find–and made some half-hearted attempts to send the curious little eavesdropper away. Thinking this a splendid sort of game, the little

black nose kept reappearing at various different points under the sides of the tent. Finally books and clothing were thrown in all directions until, at last, victory was proclaimed by the campers, and Jess realized she was opposed by superior forces. Admitting defeat is not a natural badger characteristic. Jess beat a retreat, only to resume battle again the next night, but she found a much better defence had then been organized.

For the whole time she was staying with us, Gabrielle remained rather nervous of Jess. In fact, I think she never really appreciated having the badger around the house. Late one evening, when she and Joanna were in the swimming pool Jess, attracted no doubt by the noise they were making, arrived beside the pool. The girls were at home alone at the time, and as there was no point in shouting for help, the acquatic sports were prolonged rather longer than they had intended. When, at last, the bathers thought the coast was clear, they quickly scrambled out and grabbed their towels before rushing for safety. Jess's idea, of course, had been to lay an ambush. This thoroughly scared Gabrielle, who shouted, 'Get zis badger away,' as she jumped on to Joanna's back. Joanna, finding herself saddled with an unexpected burden, staggered towards a near-by garden seat, but it proved to be no sanctuary and was quickly abandoned as they both dashed on to the house. Once safely in the kitchen, Gabrielle leapt on to the table and left Joanna to deal with the badger on her own.

By then Jess had gone upstairs, where a Spanish girl, who strongly disapproved of both badgers and late-night swimming, had gone to bed early. Of course, it wasn't long before Jess badgered at her door, which prompted a shout of 'Please make less noise Joanna – I am sleeping,' but it was some time before Joanna could coax the over-excited badger back into the garden and firmly shut all the doors.

When Gill and I returned some half-hour later, we found Gabrielle still sitting on the kitchen table placidly reading her book. After she had returned to France, she sent us a long and amusing letter thanking us for her holiday, but what her sisters and parents were told about 'Jassy', as she always called the cub, we could only guess.

'The first time I saw Jassy,' she wrote later, 'was for dinner round the table. I thought she looked quite nice but unfortunately she did eat my shoes so I realized she was very dangerous. I was only a little bit frightened, and became used to her in the end and was considering her presence in the house as a typical example of the English way of life.'

As time went on, other news of Jess's nefarious nocturnal activities gradually reached us. It appeared she was sometimes seen playing with local dogs; she was suspected of having dug out two wasps' nests and of leaving not a little mess in somebody's garden. Wasps' nests are often dug out by badgers, who like the grubs, and I was very keen to see Jess at work on one. Alas, when the site of a third wasps' nest was reported and offered to her one night, she expressed no interest whatever and declined to perform before a large crowd of onlookers armed with cameras and flashlights.

I sometimes wondered if our other near farming neighbour, Basil Crisford, who had actually been born at

Old Farm Place, lamented the day his grandfather had sold the house. Since those days it had been filled with a succession of marauding children who kept a variety of different animals. Basil and his wife Grace must often have wondered what they might expect next in the way of unusual events and unorthodox livestock. Luckily Basil was blessed with a keen sense of humour and nothing ever seemed to ruffle him. This was just as well, for Jess later took to visiting his farm quite regularly, and even to badgering their back door.

Among our neighbours to whom I was most anxious to introduce Jess, were the three Miss Blumfields, owners of Shawland Farm, which seemed ideal badger territory and whose wood contained the nearest genuine badger sett to our property. Kathleen and Muriel Blumfield ran the farm in the tradition of their parents before them, milking their herd of Guernsey cows by hand, while their younger sister Beryl kept house. The sisters had no electricity or machinery of any sort and always used oil lamps in the house. I knew they were often to be found working late in their dairy, so, with Jess and the Bully, I called on them one evening. News of my rearing a badger cub had evidently reached them by bush telegraph, so they were not particularly surprised to meet me with Jess. I think Kathleen and Beryl were amused at the thought of having a half tame badger around, but Muriel, who was responsible for their poultry–large flocks of which could always be seen wandering about the farmyard unpenned as in former days–was not quite so pleased. She knew all about badgers and that they often visited their farm at night, but were very rarely seen and she had recently heard of one which had had to be destroyed for killing one of her friend's bantams. It didn't therefore seem quite the moment for me to recount to them Jess's experiences with our own bantams; so I said no more, hoping she would never seek that sort of amusement on their farm. At all events, I noticed that she was frightened of their turkey cock and their geese, which were outside the cowshed at the time, and which, like guinea fowl, make excellent farmyard watchmen.

7
A BADGER AT LARGE

As homeward through the lane I went with lazy feet,
This song to myself did I oftimes repeat;
And it seemed, as I retraced the ballad line by line,
That but half of it was hers, and the other half of it was mine.
William Wordsworth

Unfortunately our garden and fields were bordered on one side by a road which often carried more traffic than we liked, while on the other there ran a narrow lane. Somehow Jess would have to be taught never to linger on a road, and as an elementary lesson I often took her along the side of the hedge adjoining the road. I was relieved to notice how passing traffic would drive her instinctively in towards the centre of the field. This was an encouraging sign. Nevertheless, cars and tractors were a hazard she would one day have to experience on her own in more vulnerable conditions. I thought of repainting a notice 'Beware of Children', which the previous owners of our house had once displayed, to read 'Beware of Badgers', but felt it would perhaps give an equally sinister and misleading impression.

Meanwhile my evening rambles with Jess were giving me an unrivalled opportunity to study at leisure the habits of badgers which I had previously only observed from a distance.

A badger's main sense is derived from its extraordinary ability to detect different scent. This seems miraculous to us humans, who, by comparison, have a relatively poor sense of smell. Scent is, of course, all-important to many animals since it is their main means of finding food. It is said that a badger can, for example, detect a nest of young rabbits at the surface from directly above, and so dig it out with unerring accuracy. Jess could detect an earthworm that was well below the surface, and she could follow up my scent or that of the Bully, no matter where we might have gone, long after we had passed over the ground. I think she could even tell from outside the garden door whether is was me or someone else she knew who was in the house. She often musked my shoes (and those of anyone else to whom she took a fancy) in the same way that badgers do to other members of their clan, but I am sure it was my personal scent to which she was attracted. Priscilla and Joanna, of course, maintained that it was because I swam a lot in the summer, which led them to argue that I did not have enough hot baths.

Whatever the reason, I often tried, seldom with success, to give Jess the slip when we were together on a walk. When I did succeed in losing her, it was interesting to see through binoculars what she did about it. She would first search frantically for any muskings made on the outward journey, and sometimes even that did not seem to work. Then she would show signs of panic and start to cast wildly around. At that point, soft-heartedly, I would always relent and go to her rescue. It is difficult to say when her homing instincts became fully developed. She must have roamed quite widely from an early age, but was always back in her garden sett before sunrise.

Jess disliked cows and sheep, even when they were only standing still or lying down. I presumed this must be because she found their smell unpleasant or thought that the noises they made gave an indication of danger. I had noticed the same aversion to cattle among wild badgers, and so think it most unlikely, as has occasionally been suggested, that they could ever be held responsible for killing lambs. There have been suspicions that badgers, like other animals and birds (especially starlings which are often to be seen with cows) may be responsible for spreading tuberculosis among cattle on certain farms in the West of England. This is something that is still subject to investigation by experts since predatory animals, like badgers, are normally immune to such infections or they would have long ago been wiped out. Nevertheless, it appears that some families of badgers in a small part of Gloucestershire and Wiltshire and in Cornwall have become infected with bovine tuberculosis; presumably from having consumed an excessive quantity of contaminated food from fields which have somehow been infected with the disease. Normally ill health among wild animals has to be left to nature to cure for herself, but action is invariably taken when it affects the interests of human beings and it would appear that the infected colonies in those areas may be faced with extermination. Such is man's domination of his environment. However, all the indications are that this is a local rather than a national problem and it should not be taken as an excuse for a general attack on a harmless species of wild animals, simply because a few of them may be suffering from a disease acquired as a result of his activities. Although badgers have no respect for farm boundaries, it could be argued that, given sufficient time, they might cure themselves or even rid the area of infected earth worms and dung beetles, the remains of which they would normally deposit in hedgerows and woods, where cattle do not feed; only rarely does one find a badger's latrine in open fields.

Rebecca was completely indifferent to Jess, just as she was to the dogs, but the natural curiosity of cows sometimes led them to chase Jess as they would a dog. The most successful way I discovered of putting Jess off my tracks was actually to stand still for a few minutes in the middle of a herd of cattle, when she could neither see, hear nor scent me. She would then immediately shuffle off back the way she had come, or perhaps make for the nearest cover, where she would probably remain, if she didn't know the area, until the Bully or I turned up to lead her back to more familiar territory. Jess clearly relied on us, as she would have done on her mother, to give her confidence when moving about on strange ground.

When excited or at play, badger cubs can skip like lambs, on all four legs at once. Their long claws also enable them to climb quite easily, but Jess was always reluctant to jump down from any height and preferred to scramble, presumably for fear of stubbing her sensitive nose.

Badgers communicate with each other by making a variety of different noises. These vary from low grunts, or a sort of purring sound, to a sharp, gruff bark of alarm. An excited high-pitched cackle is made particularly by cubs when playing or scrapping together, while a badger's scream of pain or anguish sounds terrible to the human ear, though is very seldom heard. It has also been suggested that their scream may also have some kind of territorial or mating significance. When on a walk, Jess would snort quite frequently, as if clearing her nose; and often snapped her jaws for no reason that I could discover. When asking for food, she sometimes made the low purring noise. As a rule, however, badgers are very silent in their movements, though they can make quite a lot of noise as they go scratching around. They then seem quite oblivious to any other sound and at such moments it is possible to get quite close to them–provided, of course, you can do so up wind.

For a long time water that wasn't in her drinking bowl seemed strange to Jess, and the first time we crossed a stream on a walk she ran for a while madly up and down the bank from which I had jumped before she could summon sufficient courage to wade across. Badgers can swim easily, but I never saw Jess do so. Once the delights of paddling about in water were discovered, however, she ceased being in the least worried about getting wet, and would shake water from her coat like a dog. Indeed she seemed to thrive in rain, presumably because it brought earthworms to the surface and slugs out of hiding. Late one night Priscilla threw a can of water over Jess from her bedroom window, to discourage her from badgering the back door long after bedtime. She said Jess calmly looked up, obviously enjoying the unexpected shower, but went on badgering the door and even seemed quite pleased at receiving a second dowsing.

The danger of Jess falling into our small homemade open-air swimming-pool was for a time an anxiety, but after she had found me splashing about in it on several occasions, she evidently agreed with the Bully–who hated getting wet and never drank the water because of the chlorine–that the pool was in a part of the garden better avoided on the whole.

By early August, things seemed to have gone so well that I decided to introduce Jess to the genuine badger sett in Shawland Wood. Although this had been in existence for many years, it had fallen into disuse until being extensively renovated the previous winter. I was fairly confident by then that it had no permanent residents and the risk of a badger being within when Jess paid it a visit was one that would have to be taken. She already knew the paths in the wood that were used by visiting badgers, and had liberally musked them for herself, but on the first two or three occasions when we went to the sett, Jess showed very little interest and even appeared slightly nervous. She declined to go further down than head and shoulders, but later did not hesitate and went the whole way, albeit gingerly and with obvious caution. Reappearing a few minutes later out of the same hole, she then thoroughly inspected the surrounding area. This seemed satisfactory to be going on with, so I left it at that, but continued to include that part of the wood in our evening walks and on several occasions left her a midnight feed close by the sett.

Towards the middle of the month, I had a feeling that Jess was no longer spending the days in her garden sett. She was not about the garden in the evenings, and was only found when I had gone down to the wood, where she came readily when called. She was, as always, eager to join in my walks, but had become noticeably more at ease in the woodland, where she was prepared to snuffle about on her own and would return less frequently to make sure I was still around. We knew she continued her visits to the house after we were in bed, for the gale continued to sweep through the summer house before morning.

As I am not usually at home on week-days, I had to wait for the weekend before finding out whether or not my suspicions were correct. At midday one sunny Sunday morning I set out for an investigative exp ition to Shawland Wood with the Bully, who had a sore paw at the time, and was not as bustling as usual. The Bully knew the wood and the sett, with its several different entrances, extremely well, and while she was busy on other matters, I quietly approached the hole Jess had used previously and softly called her name. To my joy, within half a minute out came a familiar little snout and then Jess was looking at me as much as to say, 'Yes, I'm here, what do you want?' She didn't seem particularly sleepy or put out at being roused, so I guessed she was probably still feeling a little insecure. I gave her a scratch, she musked my shoe, exchanged noses with the Bully. Then, thinking that was enough, I wished her 'Good day'.

The sett was at the far end of the wood away from the Shawland Farm, but only about a hundred yards from Basil Crisford's house. It therefore seemed a courtesy to go over to inform him and his wife Grace of the arrival of their new neighbour.

I left the Bully to her own devices in the wood, as she and Basil's golden labrador bitch had a long-standing feud. The fur flew pretty freely whenever they met, and I could only hope there would not be similar objections should she ever meet Jess on the farm which she clearly regarded as her own.

'You've got a new neighbour, Basil,' I said, 'less than a hundred yards from your back door.'

'Oh yes?' said Basil in his phlegmatic way. 'Now I

know who's been running off with my gumboots every night, and what's been making our Honey bark her head off.'

'I hope you haven't lost them?' I asked, fearing I might have to buy him another pair of boots.

'Oh no,' he said, 'they're always somewhere in the orchard, and it's not difficult to find them before I go out milking.'

It seemed that Basil, weary after his day's labour and tired of keeping the peace with Grace, who never failed to mutter when he took his boots off in the kitchen and scattered hayseeds everywhere, had acquired the habit of leaving them in the porch outside the back door, where they invariably stayed till needed in the morning. Little did he know that gumboots were for Jess second only to curtains on her list of favourite playthings. Luckily a sense of fun appealed to Basil's humour, so Jess's antics, which could have provoked wrath and vengeance in other people, caused him nothing but amusement.

Returning some twenty minutes later to make sure that all was well, it was touching to find the Bully lying as self-appointed guardian to the hole down which Jess had evidently resumed her interrupted slumber. I think the Bully's feelings were as mixed as mine, for the time was clearly coming closer when ours and Jess's ways would finally separate.

Later that afternoon it occurred to me that Jess's new home would probably be very spartanly furnished, so I went back with an armful of hay, which I dropped casually near by. This small gesture was obviously appreciated for it had all been taken in when I looked that evening.

We must presume that much of a badger's life underground is spent in sleep as they take a lot of trouble to see that their beds are clean and comfortable. In doing this, badgers collect large quantities of suitable dry material, such as hay, grass, bracken, leaves and even small twigs. This they transport between their fore-paws, the bundle being tucked closely under the chin as they shuffle backwards towards and down their sett. Once underground, all the material gathered is formed into a neat and cosy nest, which is frequently changed when the weather permits, particularly in the early spring and late summer. Discarded bedding, which sometimes contains badger hairs, may often be found outside the entrance of setts in use.

We had reached a notable turning-point in Jess's life. She had been successfully fostered and weaned by the Bully, on whom she was no longer so dependent, and had now moved of her own accord one step nearer to the wild. She still had several lessons to learn, but there seemed little more for me and the Bully to do. For her part, the Bully remained friendly, but often showed embarrassment at being closely followed by a badger, on which she would even sometimes turn in anger should Jess become over-familiar. The Bully was, of course, unusual, but I suspect that there is no natural antagonism between badgers and dogs, who have often had to be encouraged to attack them. A friend of mine, who had many badgers on his farm, often used to see them exchanging greetings with his sheep dogs before each went about their own business. Jess still had to learn for herself, however, that human beings and their dogs might be hostile. There was little we could do about this ourselves, so it would have to be one of those things she must find out for herself. Now that she was weaned from the Bully, it only remained to wean her from the house and myself.

The question that then arose was when, and by how much, should we reduce the food we gave her? By her grubbing about I knew she was making progress in finding food for herself, but was reluctant to cut off our supply completely until she was more or less full grown. We therefore decided we would, from then on, only provide food for Jess on the terrace of the house, which, being partially covered by wisteria, was generally known in the family as the 'wisterianda'. The garden door led out to the wisterianda and so we would be able to keep a check on what Jess ate and make sure that neither the dogs nor other animals got to it first. In any case, I came to the conclusion that food left about in the wood could provoke a fight with other badgers.

Jess had grown noticeably more aggressive when eating her food. She would still allow me to scratch her as she fed, but would brook no interference from anyone else and would repel the dogs fiercely if they came too close. Needless to say, there was a two-way understanding about this, as the dogs, for their part, did the same to Jess when they were feeding. She certainly had a voracious appetite and consumed all that we offered: when I did begin to cut down her food towards the end of August, it was by including less puppy meal and vegetable. I felt that cutting off the small amount of meat we gave her could unwittingly have encouraged Jess to turn her attention on our neighbours' cat or dog food, or even back to Gill's bantams.

One evening Jess arrived quite early on the wisterianda with what both Gill and I thought was a distinctly malevolent look in her eye. She was evidently bored, and, having found little to amuse her once she had had her supper, must have decided to inspect the possibilities of fun with the bantams. She was presumably delighted to discover the gate to their stockade unlatched.

Alas, a coop containing a Pekin cock and hen had also been left open. Excited bantam cackling brought Gill and me, with the Bully and Trottie, hot-foot from the house to find Jess teasing the agitated cock. No harm was done, however, apart from the loss of a tail feather or two. Jess was by then no lightweight to lift and it needed two hands, but she raised no objection and was quite amiable at being hastily removed. The episode, so far as she was concerned, had served its purpose; it had provided activity, attention and company, even though none of us were particularly overjoyed or co-operative. The dogs especially looked most embarrassed, and gave Jess a distinctly cold shoulder. However, the cat happened to be around at the time, so he came in for a quick chase up a tree before all returned to normal and Jess stumbled off in search of other diversions.

Soon after Jess had taken up residence in Shawland Wood and become more independent in her ways, the Bully was eager for a walk one evening, so we went together to see if all was well. There was no sign of Jess at first, but while we were standing close to the sett in the gloom, along came a little white head, just showing as it pushed through the thick carpet of ivy that covered that part of the wood. She greeted me as usual, and proudly showed the Bully all over her new home before making it clear she would like to accompany us on our walk.

After that I resisted the temptation to go down to the wood for the next few nights, and went my evening walks alone or with the Bully. Once, when we were going together quietly down the lane which cuts through Shawland Wood, I looked up to see Jess sitting high on a bank. She hadn't seen us, so we stood for some time, quietly watching as she groomed herself and snuffled about generally, seemingly quite happy to be on her own. Suddenly she raised her nose, having obviously caught mine or the Bully's scent, but it was quite some time before she eventually found us in the lane and, having greeted us with usual gusto, joined in the walk.

It was a lovely summer evening, and since Jess seemed particularly energetic, rushing frantically all over the place, I decided to go further than usual and introduce her to an entirely new area. We crossed several fields, one of which contained a large herd of bullocks which the Bully, true to her nature, attempted to scatter. The resulting noise and stampede thoroughly alarmed and sobered Jess, who instantly stopped wandering and stuck close to my heel. By the time we emerged through a gate on to a road she had completely recovered from her jitters, when, to my consternation swiftly round a bend shot a large fast car. Fearing disaster, and knowing Jess would be terrified by its headlights and noise, I waved to the driver to stop. At this Jess fled in panic down the road, occasionally glancing backwards. I quickly explained the situation to the driver and his passenger, whose expressions registered a mixture of disbelief and pity at finding such an eccentric countryman wandering after dark with an unleashed bull-terrier and a badger on the Queen's Highway–meant, of course, for the exclusive use of the internal combustion engine. Even so, the driver kindly heeded my request and drove off carefully, loudly sounding his horn,

leaving me–or, more accurately, the Bully–to track Jess down some while later, deep in a strange wood with her morale and composure seemingly restored.

Many badgers are killed each year on England's roads This is in part because of their extraordinary persistence and determination, which has become proverbial. They will keep going in a specific direction or stick to a traditional path regardless of obstacles. This has led the Forestry Commission to fix special badger gates in some of its wire fencing, and the highway authorities to provide special tunnels under newly constructed motorways in rural areas. It is just as well.

Jess's encounter with the car, however, had fortuitously provided the lesson I had long wanted to arrange, but had not been able to think how it might be devised safely. Later that night, as we wended our way home, I was glad to note that Jess recrossed the road as quickly as she could with obvious care. So I hoped that the little incident would prove an experience she would remember all her life. Maybe it would provide a useful subconscious safety reflex.

Towards the end of August Jess evidently had another encounter with a wild badger. Late one evening, as Andrew and I were swimming in the pool, there came a lot of badger noises from the field across the valley. They didn't sound particularly ominous or vicious, though the Bully, who was in the garden at the time, immediately set off to join the fray. As we were clad only for swimming we didn't venture forth ourselves, having the brambles in mind. We reckoned Jess was by then old enough to fight her own battles and the fact that the Bully had gone to act as a reinforcement seemed to us to be enough. The scrap, if that was what it was, did not last long, and all was quiet by the time I had put on some clothes and gone over to investigate. There I found Jess with the Bully carrying out what looked like one of their routine patrols. When Jess joined us later on the wisterianda, however, Andrew and I noticed that Jess was bleeding slightly from a little bite just above the tail. She declined to let us examine the wound, but as she seemed quite unconcerned, we left her alone and went indoors to bed. It was over a week before Jess would let me scratch that part of her back, where there were several obvious little scabs.

Jess's time of arrival on the wisterianda became steadily more erratic. Sometimes she would arrive quite early in the evening, and on other occasions it would be long after we had gone to bed. Her food continued to be left out, however, and I was always apprehensive when I heard a car travelling fast down the lane.

Our son Hugh, who was my greatest badger ally in the family and had not yet met Jess, came home to spend the last weekend in August. To celebrate this, we once again let her have the complete run of the house. Jess gladly accepted the open invitation, and happily revisited all her favourite haunts, particularly upstairs in the girl's bedrooms. It was like old times for her: she wrapped herself in any curtains within reach, explored the sitting-room and turned out all the dirty clothing and shoe polish she could find in the laundry. By then Trottie's pups were gone, so we were allowed to have a badger in the kitchen at suppertime, where she clambered over an unprotesting Bully, who was lying by the Aga, liberally musking her as she did so. That was, after all, the only way she had of expressing her appreciation. Jess played with Trottie and ruffled up her bed, and climbed up on my lap to see what I was having for supper. Later we gave her her food on the wisterianda and said, 'Good night,' but she was still in the garden when I took the dogs out later. No doubt she was reviving other youthful memories.

That weekend we noticed that there were signs of extensive digging outside one of the holes of the sett in Shawland Wood. It looked to me suspiciously like the work of a dog, but was most unlikely to have been done by the Bully or Trottie. Jess did not come up when I called, so thinking it was possible she might have moved further away, my sons and I carefully made an inspection of all the other badger setts in our immediate neighbourhood. There was no evidence that any of them were in use, so we assumed that Jess must by then have been sleeping more soundly than she had at first. Perhaps, we thought, she didn't want to be disturbed, and this was subsequently confirmed by watching later that evening, when she emerged rather sleepily from a different part of the sett. She had obviously moved her quarters to a deeper and probably more secure chamber on account of the digging by the dog. This seemed a wise precaution and showed how Jess was at last developing a more sophisticated sense of self-preservation.

8
A PLACE OF HER OWN

The melancholy days are come,
The saddest of the year,
Of wailing winds and naked woods,
And meadows brown and sere.
William Cullen Bryant

Life could not have been easy that year for the wild badgers in East Sussex. We had had near-drought conditions for most of the summer, and the ground was unusually hard and dry. The harvest was all home before the end of August. This must have made as much difference to the lives of the badgers as the sudden felling of a forest would seem to us. It would also alter the character of many fields, in which much of their food is found. During the autumn months, badgers consume large quantities of earthworms to fatten themselves up for the approaching lean months of winter. I noticed from her dungpits that Jess occasionally ate a little corn, but it was never completely digested.

The evenings began to draw in noticeably during September. Usually a month of great activity for badgers. It is said to be the time when the different badger families, formed the previous season, begin to split up, thus preventing inbreeding. I thought there might, in consequence, be much coming and going rather earlier than is usual between the two main colonies in our vicinity, on the edge of whose territories Jess had established her own.

There was also a chance that she might have become a little more willing to fraternize with other members of her species and would have ceased to treat her visitors with the obvious hostility she had till then displayed.

It therefore seemed important that the Bully and I should be careful to avoid contact with her as much as possible, leaving her alone to do as she pleased without the undue distraction of our presence. The Bully was still glad to sniff noses with Jess from time to time, but was no longer particularly interested in having her around; once again she was busy terrorizing the grey squirrels, which were then becoming very active gathering all the hazel nuts in the woods, and stripping unripe walnuts and fruit from our garden.

So far as I was concerned, my only contact with Jess, who still musked my shoes whenever we met, lay in giving her a friendly little scratch from time to time. This was something she appreciated, and even appeared to expect in return for her squatting on my shoes. I rarely picked her up, but on more than one occasion Priscilla and I had to remove ticks from behind her ears. This was one thing Jess seemed unable to do for herself, and may be one of the reasons why badgers are sometimes seen industriously grooming each other. Ticks grip their victims in their jaws and suck their blood, in the process often swelling to large proportions. Then, if they are roughly removed, their heads get left behind, and will often cause festering sores. The easiest way of making a tick relax its grip completely is by gently touching it with a lighted cigarette. However, this is not very easily achieved in the ear of even a friendly badger, and I am afraid Cilla and I were not always successful in our efforts.

It was a great pleasure to see Jess on those last few evenings in August, when she still came regularly to the wisterianda for her food. By then she was almost full grown, weighed nearly twenty pounds and had a beautiful dark shiny coat. Her mouth was full of splendid teeth and her fore-claws were both long and sharp. She was obviously very fit and strong for her age, and a most attractive specimen of her species. So she should have been, being probably the best-fed badger in the county that year.

The rain came towards the middle of September. It was just in time to revive the parched pastures, so badly needed by the farmers to feed their cattle and sheep, many of which were brought up to our area from the near-by marshes to spend the winter on higher ground. Jess had developed plenty of other interests, and was no longer paying us regular nightly visits. Walking in the garden late one evening, enjoying the sweet smell that rain brings after a prolonged dry spell, I thought I heard the sound of badgers playing, coming from the valley where Jess had had her first fight, which made me wonder whether all was going well. Had Jess decided to become more sociable, I thought? There was no point in trying to find out, or in interfering in what were strictly her private affairs; anyway, I felt quite confident that she was well able to look after herself by then and was particularly anxious not to scare any wild badgers away.

My curiosity, however, got the better of me, and a few nights later I went by myself down to Shawland Wood to see if Jess was still around. After quietly watching her sett through binoculars for a while, and seeing nothing, I cautiously approached it up wind. Everything was silent, so I softly called Jess by name. There was an immediate rustling in the brambles that surrounded the furthest entrance, and a badger appeared. It came hesitantly in my direction until it recognized my scent. It was, of course, Jess, but her greeting was noticeably subdued and she seemed a little suspicious at seeing me. She sniffed rather casually at my shoes, but did not musk them; let me scratch her back and ears and gladly accepted a little chocolate from my hand, but showed no desire to join me in a walk, or even to leave the vicinity and seemed strangely alert, as if keeping an ear cocked for something in the direction of the sett. This made me wonder whether she was, in fact, already sharing it with another badger; if so, my presence was probably constituting an embarrassment.

To try and establish a similar amicable relationship with a completely strange animal would be a very difficult thing to achieve, requiring immense care and patience. A wild badger must first grow accustomed to your scent, and then come to associate it with something pleasant. Food is the natural thing with which to curry favour: cooked meat, bacon rinds, bread with honey, or raisins are among the most acceptable things I know, but any sudden movement will cause instant alarm. I was strongly tempted to try to see whether I could at least woo the interest of Jess's friend, but then decided it would be most unwise; it might scare them both away. I therefore withdrew quietly and left her, alone in the dark, going slowly back towards the sett.

For the next week or so the Bully and I only visited Shawland Wood from time to time and never went near to the sett. The Bully was, in any case, far more interested in the trees at the other end. From an inspection of the latrines near the sett, it appeared that more than one badger might be using them and this seemed a satisfactory omen.

The land across the valley from our house belonged to Mike Bowman, who always put down a lot of hand-fed pheasants and that year had reared quite a number of young partridges as well. On account of his concern for the safety of his game, I had never taken Jess for walks over the farm though we knew, from her visits to the Linns, that she must occasionally have gone in that direction. Pheasants roost at night and would not usually hold any interest for a badger, but I was not sure about the partridges. They congregate in coveys and sleep on the ground and there was always a chance Jess might accidentally stumble on one in the night. I didn't want her nocturnal activities to upset my cordial relations with Mike who kindly let me wander freely all over his farm and was not unfriendly towards badgers. However, I knew he viewed my involvement with Jess with a certain amount of apprehension, and, like all farmers and landowners who are interested in shooting, he hated foxes; despite the fact that he had once landed me with a young cub to rear.

Early in September he moved his hand-reared pheasants to a specially wired enclosure in a wood across the valley, where they could learn to fly and lead a normal life. There was an old and fairly large badger sett nearby on which I knew that Mike kept a very sharp eye, in case a fox or vixen might decide to use it as a residence.

On several occasions when out badger watching, I have seen a fox pass cautiously through a sett, but never when badgers were in the vicinity. Foxes and badgers don't usually co-habit, or get on particularly well together, but I knew of one sett where a vixen with cubs occupied one end in apparent amity with the badgers who lived in the main part, and once I even saw a fox come out rather hastily from the same hole from which the rightful owners themselves emerged half an hour later. This was most unusual, since badgers will normally have no truck with a fox, who respectfully keeps his distance. This rather strained relationship was vividly observed one night by a friend of mine, who like many other people in our area had for many years regularly provided a sumptuous feast for the badgers which visited her garden. She said foxes only rarely visited her badger banquet; but on one occasion a fox did turn up before the invited guests, who were a little late in arriving. Seeing the fox guzzling from their tray, two of the badgers immediately rushed forward and grabbed the intruder by the rump, throwing it into the pottage in their rage, whereupon, my friend said, the fox retired hurt and did not dare to return until after the badgers had eaten all they wanted and gone on their way.

Early one morning towards the end of September, Gill saw a young sandy-coloured fox passing beneath our bedroom window with what looked like one of her bantams in its mouth. I was shaving at the time, and not in a position to do much about it so, containing her rage in silence, she rushed downstairs and gave chase. Hearing her shout, the fox dropped its breakfast, which turned out to be someone else's chicken, and fled towards the wood. Later that same morning, Mike Bowman found Trottie, on an unauthorized expedition to his farm (she was charitably thought to have followed up the fox), but unfortunately caught her red-footed with a dead pheasant at her feet. Naturally this infuriated Mike, who, thinking he had better teach her a sharp lesson, emptied both the barrels of his gun in her direction. One in front and the other behind. This had the desired effect and sent her flying home in fright; he hoped a much wiser dog–as we did, too, when we heard about it.

When I returned home from work that evening, and heard of Trottie's misdemeanour, I went over to discuss this and the presence of the fox with Mike while he was feeding his pheasants, and naturally took the opportunity of asking if he had by any chance seen anything of Jess. The Bully was with me on a lead, and on our way home we visited the near-by badger sett, which I knew had not been in use a few weeks previously. There were obvious signs of recent digging at one of the entrances, with which the Bully became extremely interested, even excited. She might, of course, have been scenting rabbits, which had returned in large numbers to our area that summer, but the excavation looked to me more like the work of badgers, so I decided I would return by myself the next evening to watch.

The sett was in a very steep bank above a little valley which was thickly covered with trees and brambles, and though I had seen several badgers there in previous years, it was not an easy one to approach and get the wind right. It was drizzling as I arrived, and there was very little wind or light, but when still some way off I briefly but distinctly saw a young badger through my binoculars. It was looking at me out of the brambles close above the sett. After watching me suspiciously for a few seconds it bolted like thunder down one of the holes. Badgers thus alarmed or disturbed do not usually come up again for quite a long time. But, undeterred, I settled down on the bank above the sett and waited. To my surprise I was rewarded for within a very few minutes, out of the same hole down which the badger had scurried, emerged a very sleepy Jess, probably having been woken up by the noise. She was not more than fifteen feet from me, but seemed quite unaware of my presence and started to groom herself as was her custom. After a few minutes' scratching, her nose went up and, catching my scent, she looked up and saw me and quickly clambered up the bank to give me my usual little welcome.

Thus began the most fascinating and rewarding badger-watching evening I had ever experienced. It was several weeks since we had met. After musking my trousers, Jess climbed straight up on my lap. I offered her some raisins and bacon rind which she guzzled with pleasure before putting her nose in my pocket to see if it contained more. I helped her with her grooming, but was sad to see she had a slight festering sore behind one of her ears where Cilla and I had removed, obviously unsuccessfully, a tick some weeks before. Jess made it clear that she would like to have this scratched, for she continually thrust her head into my hand and let me examine it closely with my torch. It was healing all right and seemed in no way serious, but was nevertheless probably rather irritating.

During the hour or so we spent together on the bank that evening, I was thrilled to watch Jess return several times to the hole from which she had emerged, making the same little low purring sounds that she had sometimes uttered as a cub, especially when asking for food. Twice she even went grunting right down into the sett, as if trying to persuade her companion to join me on the bank and to demonstrate that there was no cause for alarm. None of this succeeded and in the end, thinking I might have overstayed my welcome, I said farewell and left for home, leaving Jess muttering and grumbling to herself on the bank.

Jess and her companion had probably found the Shawland Wood sett much too noisy, it being so close to Basil's farm. Now that they had acquired a new and altogether superior address, I thought it would be wise to inform Mike and Annette about the squatters who seemed to have taken possession of their sett. The shooting season was just beginning and I think Annette was much more thrilled than Mike.

This was the third most important event in Jess's life. Although we always hoped she might, I never thought it likely that she would make friends with a wild badger quite that quickly. Had she a boy friend or a girl friend, everyone wanted to know? I could give no answer. All that could be said for certain was that he, or she, was about the same size and appeared to be fairly young. Adult badger boars are usually slightly larger than the sows, but, unless you can look at them directly head on, their long hairy coats make them difficult to distinguish in poor light. A fully grown boar has a noticeably wider head when compared with a sow, and has a slightly thicker neck. The only certain way I know of distinguishing a male from a female is on those not infrequent occasions when they lie on their backs and groom their tummies with their fore-claws.

For the next three weeks we saw no more of Jess and were naturally sad when she no longer visited the wisterianda. I deliberately kept away from both the setts that she was using, and it seemed as though our little saga was moving towards a happy ending; but things were not to be quite that easy for Jess.

9
WINTER

Now there is frost upon the hill
And no leaf stirring in the wood;
The little streams are cold and still;
Never so still has winter stood.
George O'Neill

The newly fallen leaves of autumn make it very difficult to detect what badgers may have been up to in the night. All the other setts, to which the Bully and I resumed our weekend visits, looked unkempt and unused and in many cases leaves appeared to block most of the holes.

There was, of course, much speculation among our friends, who were unfamiliar with badger life, as to whether or not Jess might have found a mate, and if she had whether she would have cubs the next season. While there was a faint possibility that she had done so, I personally considered it to be extremely unlikely. Female badgers do not normally reach sexual maturity until they are fourteen or fifteen months old, and for males it is later still. But there may be exceptions, and Jess was undoubtedly a very forward miss for her age.

Very little is known about the social life of badgers and it cannot be said for certain whether they mate for life or are promiscuous. I imagine much depends on circumstances and whether they form a pair-bond early in life. If they do they might become monogamous, but if the clan is a fairly large one, the strongest male will almost certainly predominate, as is the case with many other animals. Despite their aggressive nature towards each other, badgers are gregarious creatures and large numbers can often be seen leading a remarkably contented communal existence. Their colonies, however, vary greatly in size, and they often use more than one sett. I have seen as many as twenty badgers all happily occupying a single sett, and one that I had often watched was almost certainly occupied one year by a single boar with three sows, each of whom had cubs of slightly different ages. It was, however, very difficult to identify which ones were the mothers, as they all mixed in together and never let their young suckle above ground in daylight. The community probably also included some of the previous year's brood, who by then would have looked fully grown. The boar took a notable interest in the whole tribe, and on the last day of July that year I saw him trying for a long time to mount a rather reluctant sow. He grew quite savage at her unwillingness to co-operate, and eventually gave it up and proceeded to cover another rather more successfully. Meanwhile the cubs and the other badgers were happily playing all around and were even getting in his way. It was altogether an extraordinary family scene: cubs can be very cheeky to their elders.

For many years the mating habits of badgers and their period of gestation remained a mystery. Then, in 1931, a German scientist named Fischer discovered that there was a delay in the implantation of the fertilized ovum (blastocyst) in badgers. Although it was well known that, at least in the south of England, cubs were always born during February or March, there was no agreement on when mating actually took place. As a result of his researches, Dr Ernest Neal concluded some years later that mating can and does occur in almost any month of the year between February and October, though fertilization is not always effected. However, irrespective of the time when mating has taken place, the blastocyst does not normally become embedded in the uterine wall of a badger sow until late November, December or even early January–the time of the year when they are least active. There is thus a period of delayed implantation, during which the fertilized ovum remains free in the uterus and this can vary from a few months, if mating took place in the autumn, to as many as nine months if it took place as early in the year as February.

Thereafter the development of the foetus is rapid and, as with other moderate-sized mammals, the cubs will be born some eight to nine weeks later, which is a time when there is often very little food about. Badgers are, however, able to store enough body fat during the summer and autumn to enable a sow to suckle her young over quite a long period, and so, by the time they are weaned, there is usually plenty of food about.

The average number of cubs in a litter in the South of England is said to vary between two and three, but four is by no means unusual. Cubs do not normally come above ground before they are six to eight weeks old, and then only in the dark, but by the time they are three months old they can be very venturesome and will often emerge before their parents in the evening.

The badger boar is believed to play little part in rearing his offspring, and I have heard it said that the sow will drive him from the sett at the time that her cubs are born. This cannot solely be due to female cantankerousness at the imminence of parturition and there must be a reason for such a banishment, which I suspect may not be very different from the instinctive reactions of rabbits at such a time. It is well known that a doe rabbit will endeavour to conceal the location of her current litter from the buck and only visit them surreptitiously for fear that, should their whereabouts be discovered, he would immediately destroy every member of it. To our thinking, nature has curious ways of preventing over-population by a species in an area and, unlike rabbits, badgers have no natural predators other than themselves. I once found a dead badger cub, which was less than a week old, outside a sett in circumstances which strongly suggested it might have been killed by another badger. There is no doubt, however, that the sow allows the boar to return later to the sett, perhaps so that he can help to keep strange badgers away and to maintain their particular family territory. In the same way, he may drive his sons out of the area once they become mature, though he probably does not object particularly to his daughters remaining, who may thus become the sort of universal aunts that one very often sees still present in large colonies, playing with the next year's brood.

One night, towards the end of October, after we hadn't seen Jess for some while, we were having supper quietly in the kitchen when there was a sudden badgering of the garden door. Joanna, overjoyed, rushed to open it, and in stalked Jess without any hesitation, just as she always used to do. We were, of course, delighted to see her, and the Bully and Trottie gave her a touching little welcome. As I hastily prepared a meal for the unexpected guest, she gaily explored the kitchen and inspected all the boots which were kept in the laundry just as though she had never been away. She even tried, but failed, to dislodge the cat from his comfortable position in the laundry basket.

As she was eating her food later in the kitchen, however, we were shocked to see what looked like an extremely nasty bite just above her tail. She would not let us investigate the wound, but it didn't seem to be worrying her unduly, and later she ragged quite happily with Trottie. Exhausted by all this activity, she then spent a long time grooming herself in the hall, where she allowed the Bully to lick her wound, since this was something she could not do herself. After being in the house for nearly an hour, she asked to go back into the night.

I watched her give the rockery a cursory inspection for slugs and snails, and then search the lawn for worms before wandering back down the lane. The garden door was again badgered in the small hours of the night, but we didn't answer. Sleepily we thought that once a night was enough, and left it to the Bully, who slept just inside and ignored the racket for a time, to shoo her away and make it clear that there were certain times when the arrival of even the most welcome visitors is inconvenient.

Jess eventually took the hint, but turned up again two nights later, when Joanna and I were in the house alone. That time we were able to have a much closer look at her wound; it had clearly been caused by a very savage bite. The jagged teeth marks were plain to see. Had Jess been a dog we would have taken her to the vet to have it stitched, but imagined his face, and the faces of his assistants, not to mention those of the owners of the cats and dogs in his surgery, if we arrived in his waiting-room and asked him to suture a badger. It may have seemed rather callous of us not to have tried to clean up the wound, but we came to the conclusion that it would be much better left alone to heal itself; and it undoubtedly would have made matters much worse for Jess had she met other badgers reeking both of us and antispetic ointment. Badgers are very thick-skinned creatures in some respects.

Everything had seemed to be progressing so well, what could have gone wrong? We knew that Jess had become friendly with at least one wild badger whom she had accepted on her own territory; it seemed most unlikely that the stranger would have suddenly turned on Jess after discovering she was friends with me. In any case, our last meeting had been weeks before. If there had been a badger fight in our vicinity, I think we might have heard it, and the only solution which seemed at all probable was that Jess must have accompanied her friend back to his or her former territory and been challenged for trespassing. Perhaps, we decided, she was walking out with a boy friend and had run into prospective in-law trouble.

Probably on account of this setback, Jess resumed her regular visits to the wisterianda, and whenever she badgered the garden door we always let her in. She was often suspicious, though, if there were strangers about, and never stayed very long. The Bully remained friendly, if a little toffee-nosed, but Jess always sought a game with Trottie in the garden before she went off again on her own. It seemed as though she was lonely and in need of company. She sometimes left in the direction of Shawland Wood, where I noticed there had been recent renovations to two of the entrances of the sett. Much old bedding had been turned out, for which I again unobtrusively supplied hay as replacement, and which was duly taken inside.

Jess's wound soon formed a scab and healed surprisingly quickly and it was more or less clean within a fortnight. Alas, no sooner had it done so that she was very badly bitten again and once more started to come to see us regularly. That time the wound didn't heal nearly so easily and looked a very nasty mess for quite a long time. This was a clear demonstration to us all of how vicious and beastly badgers can be to each other, and of the difficulties they must have, particularly when young, when trying to establish themselves among strangers. So far as Jess was concerned, however, she was far less troubled than we were, but obviously didn't like a solitary life without the company of other badgers. So once again we were able to look forward to her nightly visits. The rattle on the garden door became a pleasure that made us feel we had the best of both worlds, being able to entertain from the wild a friendly badger who never made trouble or overstayed her welcome.

10
RETURN TO THE WILD

We who were born in country places,
Far from cities and shifting faces,
Have a birthright that none can sell
And a secret joy no man can tell.
Eiluned Lewis

Jess's visits to the wisterianda again became less and less regular as winter advanced and then stopped altogether in the middle of December. We had, in fact, expected this for, while badgers do not hibernate, their activities are normally much reduced in winter when food becomes hard to find. If snow is on the ground it is possible to get a very good idea of a badger's nightly movements and where they have gone to search for food, but if it is deep or there is a long cold spell, they emerge less frequently and sometimes not at all.

The winter was unusually mild that year; we had no snow, and very little frost, but it was not until after all our Christmas guests had departed and the New Year festivities were over that the Bully and I began to resume our weekend walks. These, of course, included visits to all the local badger setts, each one of which had a deserted and forlorn appearance; as did the two which I thought Jess was using. I took a look at these from time to time, but while the Bully and Trottie always thought they knew which one she was occupying, I had to content myself with an inspection of her dung-pits. Jess was obviously all right, and that was as much as I could tell.

Late one afternoon in the middle of January, when the weather had turned extremely wet, the Bully spent an unusually long time investigating one of the entrances to the sett on the Bowman's farm. She flatly refused to come when I called; her head was well down a hole, and all that I could see was her tail quivering slightly as it stuck out of the bank. After several minutes like this, the Bully slowly backed out and, much to my surprise, was followed, nose to nose, by Jess. Though rather muddy, she seemed in remarkably good condition, but there was no sign of any companion and it seemed as if she had been occupying the sett alone. I called the Bully to heel and Jess followed her up the slippery bank to where I was standing. Fortunately I had a little food in my pocket, though found she evidently wasn't particularly hungry and seemed much more interested in meeting the Bully and me. After musking my gumboots, she tugged at my stockings and then clawed herself up one of my legs. It was a touching greeting, and I was particularly pleased to see that the wound she had when we last saw her had healed almost completely.

The Bully was especially friendly, but made no attempt to play; she seemed rather proud of herself for having found Jess and stood close beside her while she talked to me. We only stayed for a short while, and as we left for home Jess showed no signs of wanting to come with us but went back down her sett. The next evening Joanna insisted that we should once again visit the sett, so that she could see Jess for herself. We took Trottie on a lead, and once again the Bully persuaded Jess to join us on the bank; but this time she virtually ignored me and reserved all her greetings for Joanna and Trottie. As it was raining very hard, Joanna and I didn't linger long and much to our surprise, Jess didn't hesitate to follow us.

The stream in the bottom of the valley was full of water and flowing very strongly, so we had to wade across. Jess seemed very put out at finding a river, where there was normally a mere trickle, and she looked at it in apparent disgust. She showed no signs of wanting to brave the torrent and started to sniff about in a hedge. So we waved her farewell, but by the time we reached the house, she had somehow managed to catch us up.

Of course we invited her in for a meal, and for several nights thereafter, Jess paid us intermittent visits; so long as no strangers were present, she never hesitated to come indoors. On several occasions her arrival on the wisterianda was at a distinctly 'unsocial hour', and being sound asleep, we sometimes didn't hear her. But her rattling of the garden door invariably roused the Bully, who had never approved of being disturbed in the night and whose furious snarls and barks always woke us, but never worried Jess, who would go on badgering away till she got an answer.

Since the beginning of our long experience of bringing up a family and other animals, Gill and I had evolved a well-established understanding that, between the hours of 7 p.m. and 7 a.m., it was always she who knew best what action was needed. This unwritten agreement unfortunately didn't extend to the rearing of badgers, so it was I who had to get up to cope with the situation should Jess arrive in the small hours of the morning. Her greeting on those occasions could be embarrassingly friendly if I was not wearing slippers; I couldn't afford to stand around as she came in the house, for she would immediately try and musk my bare feet. Once she had paid her respects to me, Jess was always very careful to avoid giving further offence to the Bully, lying in her bed in the hall.

It seemed as though her visits were not solely in hope of food, for she often never finished what I offered, but that they were either in the nature of a courtesy call or, more likely, because she was feeling lonely and in need of company. She might, of course, have just wanted to make sure we had not gone away, but, whatever the reasons, Jess never stayed very long and, when she did decide to go, it was always in a hurry, as if suddenly remembering some urgent business which needed her attention. Once or twice I tried to follow her discreetly, but she always melted away in the darkness, and could easily shake off pursuit by entering impenetrable undergrowth.

In the middle of February, Gill and I noticed that a lot of other badgers had begun to pay frequent visits to our area and, to judge from the evidence they left, seemed to be feeding pretty well. This meant that Jess would either have to establish a friendly relationship with them, or move further away, so I was anxious to discover from which direction the visitors were coming.

Towards the end of winter, before the grass begins to grow again and the ground is still soft and wet, it is quite easy to track the movements of badgers; when moving from one field to another, or across a road, they always use the same gap in the hedge and their flat muddy feet leave noticeable paths, especially in woodland. Like dogs and foxes, badgers are in fact digitigrade (they walk and run on their toes), but in place of the former's four they have five toes, with a comparatively larger footpad. Thus badgers leave completely different pug marks from those of a dog or fox. When they are walking normally on flat ground, their hind-feet frequently step in the same place as their fore-feet, which are noticeably larger and have much longer claws that enable them to dig or climb with ease. When Jess was small, she could support her own weight with her claws curled round my fingers if I lifted her up by the fore-feet.

The badgers who were visiting our fields could have come from two different directions, and it appeared that they were coming from further up the valley. If Jess had come to terms with them, which I doubted, it seemed possible she might have joined up with them. On the other hand, the invasion of her territory by large numbers of strangers must have been most unwelcome to Jess, who would naturally be driven to extend her area in the opposite direction; where, so far as I knew, there were no badgers or occupied setts.

After the end of February, which must have seen her first birthday, we saw no more of Jess for quite a long time. The Bully maintained that she was still using the sett in Shawland Wood; this seemed to me quite likely since the one where she had spent the winter had been badly trampled by cattle and looked as if it had been temporarily abandoned. Several times I went alone to watch at night, but saw nothing. In any case, had I seen a badger it would not have proved very much, unless of course Jess happened to recognize my scent. It would have been quite impossible to distinguish her from other badgers in the dark, and calling her by name would only have scared any strange ones away, which was the last thing I wanted to do.

Naturally we missed her visits, and for a time I used to listen hopefully for that scratching and rattling on the garden door. Meanwhile any food we had prepared went, in simple justice, to either the Bully or the bantams. At least we had the satisfaction of feeling that we had more or less successfully accomplished the task that destiny had set us. Had we been more selfish and less conscientious in following the advice we were given, I very much doubt whether this story would have had a happy ending. However interested you may be in badgers, there is no point in hoping or pretending you might somehow make a reliable domestic pet out of one. Attractive and amusing as badgers are while young, like other animals they grow up very quickly and very soon develop all the special instincts with which nature has endowed them to survive as a species. Although you may persuade yourself that you don't mind having your trousers pulled and your carpets ruffled, or even a hole dug in your favourite armchair, sooner or later you will be in for trouble of some sort as their actions become more determined, as they inevitably will.

Despite the fact that it is now illegal to make a pet out of a badger, rescue operations, of which ours was just another example, are bound to be needed from time to time and it would be well for those who may become involved in rearing an abandoned cub, to recognize at once the difficulties that will lie ahead. It would be the cruellest and most irresponsible thing imaginable to rear a young badger in domestic surroundings, and then later to turn it out into the wild, simply because it has become too rough and determined to keep as a pet. In these circumstances it is absolutely essential to make some careful preliminary preparation.

It would, in my view, be equally unkind to rear a young badger and then send it off to some zoo or safari park, simply because you couldn't be bothered to give it the necessary training to enable it to return naturally to the wild. A badger's territorial instincts are far too strong for it to adapt to that kind of captivity. I know of one self-styled 'wildlife' park where a hand-reared badger was confined to a concrete pit and given only a hollow tree trunk about four feet long for a sett. There the wretched animal tried to sleep all day long, amid the litter thrown by curious visitors who had tried to wake it up. It does not need much imagination to appreciate the anguish such an environment would cause to any animal, let alone a badger with nocturnal and gregarious habits. It would have been far kinder to have had that poor animal humanely put to sleep for ever.

Much of the credit for our success with Jess was, of course, due to the Bully. I can't think what we should have done without her help; it certainly wouldn't have been half the fun. Not only had she adopted and fostered Jess at the time of her greatest need, but she had also provided all that comfort, warmth and companionship which every young mammal craves. Later she played with Jess, more or less as her mother might have done, and even tried to teach her how to fend for herself. Of course, the Bully's influence could have been inadvertently responsible for Jess having been perhaps a little too familiar when she first tried to make friends with the wild badgers and got so badly bitten. But that is a risk that all young cubs must run.

It had been a tremendous pleasure for us to watch a bitch displaying a strong protective attitude towards what must have seemed to her to be such a strange young animal. It had also been amazing to see the anxiety that the Bully had for Jess's safety on those occasions when things did not appear to be going quite as they should. I often wondered what the Bully can have thought about it all, if indeed she did much thinking. Her reactions must have been largely instinctive and she simply treated Jess as she would have treated puppies, had she been allowed to have them.

Jess, for her part, clearly appreciated all that the Bully had done for her, and had greatly enjoyed her company long after she herself had ceased to be regarded as an altogether respectable companion for a pedigree golden, smut and white bull-terrier. Yet the Bully never completely cold-shouldered Jess and would sometimes ask to go out on the wisterianda when Jess was there, so that she could sit like a devoted mother watching her offspring feeding. Actually, I suspected, she was only hoping to be allowed the swipes; nevertheless she would occasionally allow Jess to climb all over her, and even try to groom her, but any attempts to play was strictly discouraged. It almost seemed as if the Bully realized that Jess needed the company of other badgers and was thoughtfully encouraging her to go and make friends of her own. The whole episode raised the regard that my family and I have always felt, despite their peculiarities, for bull-terriers which, as a breed, have much in common with badgers. They, too, can be both playful and pugnacious and, when they want to be, equally obstinate and determined. They can also be sentimental and devoted, but must have very firm handling when young.

So far as I was concerned, the finding of Jess had been an exceptional experience. It had provided me with an unrivalled opportunity to observe at my feet all those little happenings I had previously only tried to see from a distance, and it was, above all, deeply touching to feel the absolute confidence that Jess always placed in me, no matter what my shortcomings may have been as a foster-father.

Man's cruelties towards these intriguing animals are well expressed in the indignant poem by John Clare, himself a countryman, humble born and bred. He was one of the few poets who have been moved to write about 'The Badger' and accurately records the so-called 'sport' of baiting them, that still went on until not so very long ago:

When midnight comes a host of dogs and men
Go out and track the badger to his den . . .
They get a forked stick to bear him down
And clap the dogs and take him to the town . . .

Though scarcely half as big, demure and small,
He fights with dogs for hours and beats them all . . .
He tries to reach the woods, an awkward race,
But sticks and cudgels quickly stop the chase . . .
Till kicked and torn and beaten down he lies
And leaves his hold and cackles, groans and dies.

John Clare lived in Northamptonshire and his first poems were published in 1820, but when I was a boy a badger ham was still regarded as something of a delicacy in many cottage homes.

It is as well that since the Badgers Act 1973 all this cruelty has finally become illegal. It is now an offence to have a live badger in your possession, unless you can show that you have taken it 'solely for the purpose of tending' on account of some disablement.

Today, death mainly lurks for badgers on the roads and lanes in our rapidly disappearing countryside. We had done all we could to teach Jess that it is now not man, but his ruthless mode of transport which would be her main enemy. I shall always feel a twinge of anxiety whenever I hear a car going fast down our lane, and can only pray that fate will take greater care of Jess that it did of her mother.

What of the future? Will Jess always know her name and recognize my voice? Perhaps, but it would be strange indeed if she didn't recognize my scent and that of the Bully if and when we ever meet. As the Bully and I roam the winter countryside together in the future, there will now be an added interest for us both in wondering whether Jess, and later perhaps her descendants, have recently passed that way, or are sleeping securely deep in any of the setts which we visit. On those occasions, the Bully's nose will undoubtedly tell her more than I shall ever know, but whatever happens we must both be careful to let Jess live her own life without any interference.

I only visited Jess's territory occasionally during the spring: but early in the summer, when I had resumed my

badger-watching outings, I was over at Mike Bowman's sett one evening. The wind was strongly in my favour, and as I sat on a shooting-stick, concealed among the brambles, I was thrilled to see before the darkness descended, two badgers cautiously emerge from the same hole Jess had used the previous autumn. After grooming themselves carefully for a while, one of them proceeded industriously to collect three bundles of bedding, which were duly taken down two of the holes, while the other badger remained gazing rather absent-mindedly into the gloom of the gully below.

Alas, I then inadvertently broke a twig: the lazy badger bolted and so did the busy one, but not before it had stared intently, for a few seconds, in my direction. One of them must have been Jess, for she would never have permitted strange badgers to use a sett that was on property she had acquired by conquest nearly a year before.

Later, when I was giving an account of my evening observations to Gill, who was ironing in the kitchen at the time, she said: 'Do you think she has a boy friend after all?' and then added, rather obliquely: 'How like a man to let a woman do all the housework.'

And so we knew, more or less for certain, that Jess was happily and completely wild. Of course, there will always be a warm welcome waiting, should she ever again pay a visit to the wisterianda and, if she remembers how to badger the garden door, we might even invite her into the house to mark the occasion. Once a bond of trust and friendship has been forged, it is very hard to break, but must never be abused; especially when it concerns an animal born in the wild.

Perhaps, one night, Jess will bring the other badger to see us and even, in time, her cubs. If that ever happens we will treat the event with all the humility it deserves. For me and my family it would be the greatest reward of all.